LIVING RELIGION
IN SUBUD

AN INTRODUCTION – PERSONAL AND HISTORICAL

EXTRACTS FROM BAPAK'S TALKS

EXPERIENCES AND EVIDENCES
of Subud members in different faiths

---

compiled and edited by
MATTHEW BARRY SULLIVAN

First published 1991.
Copyright by Matthew Barry Sullivan

Published by Humanus Ltd., an imprint of
Subud Publications International Ltd., Southdown House,
Golden Cross, near Hailsham, East Sussex, BN27 4AH, England

Cover design by Marcus Bolt
Typesetting by Selectmove, London
Printed by Biddles of Guildford

ISBN 0 907728 05 7

God adjusts what He gives to mankind with the age in which man is living, so that His grace to mankind, his gift to mankind, changes with man's needs and the developing nature of his life in this world.

Muhammad Subuh Sumohadiwidjojo[1]

Subud has not come to destroy religion; it has come by the Will of God, to bring harmony into all religions, so that in their totality they may represent one human family, one aim and one God. Later on you will be able to prove for yourselves the truth of this unity.

Muhammad Subuh Sumohadiwidjojo[2]

It is only if we are mature and solidly established in our faith and experience that we can fearlessly look at the beauty of another denomination, accept it, and still remain convinced of our own faith.

Metropolitan Antony Bloom

The blind religious are in a dilemma, for the champions on either side stand firm: each party is delighted with its own path.
    Love alone can end their quarrel, Love alone comes to the rescue when you cry for help against their arguments.
    Eloquence is dumbfounded by Love: it dare not engage in altercation.

Jalal-uddin Rumi

One hears a great deal about ecumenism these days. The only really important ecumenism in the world today is inter-faith ecumenism.

Bishop Trevor Huddleston

The Virgin of Peace at Medjugorje told her astonished young listeners that the nearest person to God in the parish was so-and-so. 'But she is a Muslim!' they expostulated. Our Lady Mary replied, 'I know; but it is not my Son nor I who put in the separations.'

Reported by Wain Weible

CONTENTS

CONTENTS

Frontispiece
Bapak shortly before his death in 1987

Centre illustrations
(i)   Bapak with his first wife Ibu Rumindah (d. 1936) and his
       mother Ibu Kursinah, circa 1925
(ii)   Bapak and his second wife Ibu Sumari with John Bennett
       at Coombe Springs, 1959
(iii) Top: Ibu Rahayu and Ibu Yati, Bapak's daughters;
       bottom: Congress in Cilandak, 1971
(iv)   Subud World Congress at Coombe Springs, 1961
(v)   Top left: Wilbert Verheyen, current chairman of Susila
       Dharma International; top right: Varindra Vittachi,
       former Assistant Secretary General of UNICEF and
       chairman of the World Subud Council since 1963; bottom:
       the editor with Père Albert Bescond at the monastery of
       St Wandrille, 1965
(vi)   Bapak and his main translator Sjarif Horthy at Virginia
       Water, 1983

Foreword

In composing a historical and general introduction to Subud I have found it impossible to stand back and attempt an objective survey. The words of the first Quaker, George Fox, have often sounded over my shoulder: 'You will say, "Christ says this and the Apostles say that," but what canst thou say?' Having asked others to bear witness – as in the pages entitled 'Evidences' – the least I can do is also to bear witness myself in my own words from my own experience and understanding of Subud, such as it is. I ask forgiveness, especially from my companions on the way, for anything here that is out of place or erroneous.

The most essential pages are in the section 'Bapak Speaks', a brief selection from the guidance and clarifications Pak Subuh himself gave over the years about the way of the latihan, especially in relation to religion. Experienced 'helpers' in Subud can find words to describe to enquirers what this path implies and what Subud is. They do so in a variety of ways coloured by their own experience, understanding and personality, for in Subud there is no doctrine or orthodoxy to be expounded. It is only in the words of Pak Subuh himself that the purity and totality of the unexpected gift he received from God on behalf of humanity for our age can be fully conveyed.

> *M.B.S. May 1991*
> *Nine Elms*
> *Jordans, Bucks*
> *England.*

ABOUT THE EDITOR

Matthew Barry Sullivan was born in Toronto, Canada. He was brought up in England and educated at Rugby and New College, Oxford, where he read History, and in Germany. He has worked in education and in publishing, and for twenty-two years was with the European Service of the BBC. He has been a member of Subud since 1957, and is both a Quaker and a communicant in the Church of England.

Matthew Sullivan compiled the compendium *Subud and Human Welfare* for the Eighth Subud World Congress in 1983 and in the same year published *Groundwork for Caring* (Humanus), a treatment of the first psychological seminar in Subud. His main work, *Thresholds of Peace* (Hamish Hamilton, 1979), which was translated into German, is a study of the 400,000 German prisoners-of-war in British hands as, out of the trauma of defeat, they took the first steps towards the democratic renewal of their country. For his contribution to Anglo-German reconciliation Matthew Sullivan was decorated in 1983 with the Bundeskreuz, the Cross of Merit, by the President of the Federal German Republic.

PART ONE

Introduction –
Personal and Historical

*'No man hath quickened
his own soul'*[1]

Subud arrives in the West

Surely not! How can this be?

A few of us had been waiting in the hall at Coombe Springs for a first glimpse of the unknown spiritual master from Indonesia, Pak Subuh. For a year I'd been going once a fortnight to this institute at Kingston-on-Thames which was devoted to the 'harmonious development of man', according to the system of Georges Gurdjieff. It was enticingly known as 'The Work', meaning psychological 'work on oneself'. While carrying out tasks in the garden or the house we had to observe ourselves as continually as possible in order to discover how mechanical our thoughts, feelings and behaviour were. We did exercises to give us a different perception of ourselves, like putting on a different walk from one's own. Once, having done this for several minutes, I became extremely frightened – it seemed that my usual self had ceased to exist.

We learned dances in which our limbs moved in a counter-rhythm to each other to music which I recall whenever I hear Satie's 'Gymnopedies'. In order to live more in the moment we had to practise 'self-remembering'. By these and other methods, which were essentially steady efforts of the attention and will, we would become 'conscious' human beings. But now, we understood, because of the unexpected foreign visitor, we were to be given something beyond this.

There he was, slowly and solidly walking down the stairs, an ordinary looking oriental in a light gaberdine suit and stylish tie, with short hair under a black *peci*. He might have been a prosperous businessman or senior government official. I felt let down. Admittedly, the brown man had a certain dignity and a pleasant smile, but that hulking figure at his shoulder, a real bruiser type . . . his assistant? It couldn't be!

An hour later every misgiving was washed away. Some ten of us, men only, stood in a half-darkened room with the two men from Java and John Bennett, director of the Coombe Springs institute. We were told to close our eyes, some simple words were spoken, telling us to open our feelings to the greatness of God and to disregard our thoughts and everyone else. Then I heard a sort of chanting and other noises. After a while I felt a slight tingling through my body. My arms started to move upwards and outwards

5

without my willing it. Somehow I trusted what was going on, but didn't understand it. After half an hour – it seemed much shorter – the word 'finish' was spoken. I opened my eyes. Two of us were lying on the floor. There was a strange, tangible peacefulness in the room. Pak Subuh was smoking a cigarette. I had been 'opened' in Subud. Something in me had been quickened.

During the following twenty-four hours I felt a quiet inner glow, akin to – but deeper than – the sense of wonder on the day after I had ceased to be a virgin. Together with being born and meeting my wife, my opening was the most important event in my life. It was also a new confirmation in my own religion. Two of those who had opened me were Muslims, yet part of the quickening process was to tell me at once to commit myself fully as a Christian. Having been an 'attender' at Quaker Meeting for some years, I at once applied to become a full member of the Society of Friends.

During that summer of 1957, with much less preparation and formality than soon became necessary, the first flush of 'openings' took place. The atmosphere at Coombe Springs was transformed dramatically. The former self-conscious wariness fell away, earnest faces relaxed. Seekers on other paths turned up. A light, joyous and optimistic feeling pervaded the place, spreading from Bapak, his wife Ibu and his party who resided for many months in a wing of the big house. The 'bruiser' who opened me turned out to be Icksan Ahmed, once a famous guerilla leader. He became known among us as the 'laughing saint'.

One day Bapak was giving a talk to some hundreds of us in a big temporary wooden hut when he suddenly cut it short. He would not go on, he explained, because we were thinking too much. It was true. From our Gurdjieff training we were centred in our heads, observing or trying to remember ourselves, and so blocking what was addressed to our quiet inner feelings. It was a simple lesson on the difference between what was happening now and what had gone on before.

But for me the main contrast was bigger than this, something that had been missing until then at Coombe Springs. I can still see Pak Subuh during a talk leaning towards us as he waits for the interpreter to finish. He seems to be absorbing, as he gazes around from the dais, the kind of people we are. What did he see in us westerners, I wondered? What I briefly glimpsed in him, and sensed from him, was love.

Who was Pak Subuh?

His full name was Muhammad Subuh Sumohadiwidjojo – for short, Pak Subuh. ('Pak' or 'Bapak', meaning 'father', is the normal address for a respected older man in Indonesia.) He was born, the eldest of four children, at dawn – Subuh means 'dawn' – on 22 June 1901 in the village of Kedungjati, a railway junction and depot in central Java. He died in 1987, outside Jakarta, immediately after his eighty-sixth birthday.

Java, once the main island of the Dutch East Indies, possesses a rich ancient culture watered by religious streams from Hinduism, Buddhism, Islam and Christianity, all of which have existed tolerantly side by side, a toleration which is uniquely enshrined in the Indonesian constitution of 1947. On both sides of Pak Subuh's family there were high-born and saintly ancestors, but under paternalistic colonial rule there was little chance of personal advancement. Subuh's father, Chasidi, like other relatives, worked for the railway, fretting under the exploitation of his country's wealth and manpower. His deeply pious mother, Kursinah, the stronger character, had visions prophesying that her son would be someone remarkable.

Subuh grew up in the warmth of a close knit, extended family in a benign tropical landscape, amid bamboo and teak forests, paddy fields, water buffalo and pointed mountains that had once been volcanoes. He showed early clairvoyant powers and, when still small, would say aloud at weddings whether the couple would be happy or not, so that his mother was asked not to take him to such occasions. When other boys fought, he felt inner pain, but at the age of ten was supreme at *pencak silat*, the dance-like, non-violent art of self-defence. The exceptional sensitivity and purity of his mind led to difficulties at the Christian school where he first learned Dutch. His tongue was unable to speak words that were untrue, unkind or coarse. One of the many reading passages stated that Javanese people were 'mentally inferior'. When the last words refused to come out of his mouth he was caned, and from such experiences he developed a temporary stutter.

At secondary school Subuh decided to become a doctor. Then at sixteen he had a clear dream in which he was visited by a man in black who told him that at the age of thirty-two he would be called by God. Understanding this to mean an early death, he gave up his medical hopes, left school and joined the railway as a trainee. Later he moved to the seaport of Semarang where he worked as a book-keeper, first in a trading company and then in the municipal offices. His father grew ill and died. Subuh bought a house and became the main support of his family. At his mother's wish he had abandoned a plan to work a passage to Holland and study accountancy there. He also had a natural talent in the arts for acting and singing, so that he joined a *wayang* troupe in a clown's part and became adept at playing the *gambang*, the Javanese xylophone.

In Semarang he listened to the student radicals led by the fiery Soekarno, his exact contemporary, destined to be the first President of Indonesia. but his way was not that of politics. He and his close friends were all on a spiritual path, one of them a Catholic who entered a seminary. But the gurus he visited were reluctant to take him on, divining in him a quality higher than that of other young aspirants. In his search for spiritual instruction he avoided anything to do with mystical ways or acquiring magical powers. For Subuh, the strict, direct way of Islam, of surrender to the will of God, was not to be departed from.

A proof of this came to him in 1925 when with two companions he attended an initiation ceremony being conducted by a Sufi master of the Naqshbandi school who had already told Subuh that he would receive what he sought from a source beyond the human level. The Sufi, nevertheless, indicated to him that, if he wished, he could come up for initiation. He did so in a spirit of experiment and, kneeling down, submitted himself to the touching and the prayers. Next day the effect had totally worn off, 'like footsteps in the dew which disappear when the sun shines on them'. Very soon after this the first momentous event of Subuh's life occurred, for which his birth, childhood and young manhood had prepared him.

The origin of the latihan

Weary from his evening study of accountancy, Subuh was having his usual late walk alone before going to bed. Suddenly – he has

8

on various occasions described in slightly different words what happened – there was a brilliant light above him, comparable to that of the midday sun. He looked up and instantly the sun seemed to have entered his head, then penetrated his body. He felt a strong quaking and trembling and thought at first he might be having a fatal heart attack. Reaching home, he lay down and surrendered himself to God.

He was aware of his whole frame filled with radiance, as if lit by electric filaments. This lasted a minute or less and he fell asleep. He awoke with a feeling of calm and happiness. He arose and, as usual, went his study for prayers, but to his astonishment all his actions were happening without his willing them. He did not walk but rather was made to walk. The movements and words of the morning prayer came from his body and his tongue of their own accord. Likewise, when he returned to rest it was without intention.

This was only the beginning. Night after night Subuh was awoken and responded to a power beyond his own will that directed his actions. Soon his limbs and body were being made to dance, his voice to chant and sing, first in known then in unknown tongues. It was all most strange and beyond his understanding, except he knew it must be a kind of training or exercise, in Indonesian *latihan*. There was no question of his being in trance, as he was always conscious and alert, as if a spectator at a play.

So it continued over a thousand nights. Every part of his body, inner and outer, underwent these exercises. His heart too was cleansed, his mind clarified and instructed, as many secrets of nature were unfolded to him. It was never the same twice, the only constancy being his surrender to God and acceptance of whatever happened. In daily life he found he could read clearly the thoughts and feelings of those around him. Members of his circle begged him to pass on this grace which, from the change in him, he had so clearly received, but he refused. It was not his to give. Since it came directly to him from God without any intermediary, it could only be given by God.

During that intense period of receiving this spiritual training, or *latihan kejiwaan* (from *jiwa* or soul), Subuh continued to work for the Semarang municipality and was promoted. At this time, too, he married seventeen-year-old Rumindah, niece of the *imam* of a neighbouring town, and the first of their five children, Rahayu, was born. But, if his outer life proceeded normally, his inner life, especially during his thirty-second year, was punctuated by

9

prophetic and visionary revelations. Twice a book appeared before him and the pictures came to life. On the first page the robed figure of the prophet Muhammad nodded gravely towards him. On the next page were people of different colours and races who moved each according to their own rhythms, asking God for forgiveness.

In the second book the pages were blank except for the first which invited him to ask questions. Through it he was told that there would be a world war, after which his country would be independent; later, he would travel across the world and spread the practice of the *latihan kejiwaan* to different races and nations who would all worship God together.

Overwhelmed, he wept with a sense of powerlessness. How could a man such as he, with a simple background and not much education, carry such a responsibility?

A new page opened on which was written, 'You must have faith in this revelation. Almighty God has power over all things.'

Some time later came the culminating revelation, an out-of-the-body event, a journey outside time and place. In this cosmic experience he travelled far beyond the visible world and communed with the living presences of Moses, Jesus Christ and Muhammad. This was his awaited call back to God. It was also the confirmation that what he had received was in direct line of the prophets whom he accepted and revered.

When Bapak was alive he sometimes told of these experiences in his talks, but acknowledged his hearers might well think they were listening to fairy tales: Since his death, his very short *Autobiography* has been published in which he relates these things as a factual record and with simple wonder that they happened to him.

Subuh now felt assured of the right to pass on this contact with the power of God to those who wished to receive it. It turned out to be a very simple process. It was enough for each person to quieten himself completely, while Subuh himself stood by, following his own latihan, as a witness to the sincerity of the wish of a person to receive the contact. Each person received and made spontaneous movements and sounds, but each differently. Nor did the latihan, Subuh found, depend on his being present himself. Anyone well-established in his or her own latihan could facilitate the contact for another.

The naming of Subud

Subuh, now in his mid-thirties, became 'Bapak' to his followers: the founder and father of a small movement which he nurtured, giving up all paid employment and living in poverty to do so. The movement gradually spread to other towns but, during the Japanese occupation of 1942–45, it was quiescent. In 1947 when there were some 300 members the new Indonesian government required all 'interiority' sects, or *kebatinan*, to be registered, so a name was required. Bapak and his intimates received the name SUBUD by 'testing' (see page 22).

When this name fell, so to speak, new-minted among them, Bapak was at once aware that its meaning was 'good and vast' and that it carried the sense of emptiness, wholeness, roundness, balance.[2] He also understood – but only afterwards – that it was an abbreviation of three Sanscrit words: *Susila*, or right living; *Budhi*, or the divine essence in every person; and *Dharma*, or surrender. Together they can be said to stand for 'the worship of God in a sincere and genuine way' and all that proceeds from that worship. (See glossary, page 146, for further explanations of these words.)

The spread of Subud

Among the thirty-three religious groups registered in Indonesia in 1947 Subud stands out distinctively in origin, in aim and in outer aspect. When, six years later, Husein Rofé, an English-educated Levantine Muslim and the first westerner to be opened by Bapak, first met him he had a surprise. He expected, as on being introduced to any oriental guru, to have to take him a gift, but the Javanese pupil to whom he was teaching English and who made the introduction said, 'Oh no, that's not necessary. Pak Subuh is a very modern person.' Rofé was greeted by a man taller and sturdier than the average Javanese, who smoked, smiled a lot, joked and laughed, a man dressed with quiet taste and entirely without pretensions. Moreover, he was treated – again a surprise – without awe or any fawning by those around him.

Rofé lived for a while in Bapak's house and realised he was being groomed to be a vehicle to take the latihan abroad. In 1954 he travelled to Japan where he opened the first members in a foreign country. The following year an article of his in an English spiritual paper about Subud was read by Meredith Starr, an Englishman then living in Cyprus, who wrote to him asking how he could be 'initiated'. In response Bapak sent Rofé to the West as his herald at the end of 1955. This led to the invitation and financing of the visit of Bapak himself and his party to England in May 1957, the first fruits of which have already been described.

Bapak's first stay in Europe – he also crossed over to Holland, Germany and Switzerland – lasted well into 1958. During this time some 800 men and women were opened. A key factor, causing the quick dissemination of Subud across the world, was that many who originally came to Coombe Springs for a Gurdjieff seminar returned to their distant countries as members of Subud – to Sri Lanka, India, South Africa and both the Americas.

Bapak returned home via San Francisco, Los Angeles and Sydney, and so completed the first of his numerous missionary journeys, lasting over a year. Five years later seed groups, often miniscule, of early members had been set up in sixty countries. A high proportion of those first opened, especially when they had been long in the Gurdjieff movement or had been lured by the excitement of what they misunderstood, did not stay.

During these journeys, which continued until the year before he died in 1987, Bapak travelled the equivalent of twenty-four times round the world.

To assist him in his mission he personally confirmed the appointment of his 'helpers' – those authorised to give both explanations and the contact. Bapak's talks and letters of general and personal guidance were translated and circulated. Periodicals were founded, a few books were published and committees were set up to oversee the practical side of Subud. Since the beginning, every four or five years a Subud World Congress has been held in a different country. The headquarters of the International Subud Committee likewise rotates.

After a few initial sensations the media almost entirely ignored Subud, just as Subud ignored the media. For in 1959 at the first International Congress held at Coombe Springs Bapak had laid down a fundamental principle:

> To spread Subud by means of propaganda simply because we live in the age of propaganda is not the way. Propaganda is today used everywhere, but people are becoming tired of it. They see that one

may be a clever talker but incapable of practising what one talks about. One can speak of riches without oneself becoming rich, one can also talk about how to be a good man and pure in heart and about how to behave in order to possess the qualities that one ought to have, but without experiencing any change of nature in this direction within oneself. Such claims are boring for people to hear and Subud should not, therefore, follow that way. Just do your work while in Subud so that it can become an example. We should not make use of propaganda, but there should be evidence in ourselves for others.

In the same talk Bapak gave a striking image of who he was:

> In all this, Bapak's function is that of a school servant who sets out the books, opens the door, cleans the room and arranges the tables and chairs. When you are all in the classroom the teacher will come and give the lessons, and the teacher is not Bapak but God Himself. Bapak is not a teacher but only a servant of God. This in truth is Bapak's position in this spiritual work of Subud, under the power of God and in His hands.[3]

What is Subud?

It is clear that Bapak is very far from being in the mould of those eastern gurus or esoteric masters who during this century have made such an impact on the West. Nor can Subud be said to be among the so-called 'new religions', though numbered among them in Jacob Needleman's well-known book by that name. Subud is not a sect, though it may seem to possess at present some of the features of a sect. There are no specific teaching, indoctrination, mantra or secret words of initiation. There is no required down-payment, nor any fee – the gift of God is free. All contributions to the cost of premises, organisation and the like are voluntary.

An applicant to Subud has to wait, normally, for three months, as a test of sincerity and to discourage mere curiosity. This also gives time for the person to be properly informed of what Subud is, and ensures their commitment. Those with a history of mental illness are not accepted because we do not yet have the specialised places in which to look after them, or because, in some cases, the power of the latihan would aggravate the illness.

Again and again, in 1700 recorded or documented talks to members, Bapak used to remind us of the qualities needed so as to obtain the full benefits of the latihan: sincerity, patience and surrender to God. The last is the most difficult. Once in Posnan a young Polish poet found a problem in my explanations. 'But we Poles do not like the word surrender.' I told him to think of it as 'letting go of self' – as saying to God, 'Here I am, Lord, at thy service.' But he wasn't a believing Catholic, didn't understand and didn't ask to be opened.

When this contact with the power of God (or Great Life as Bapak sometimes called it) occurs, an inner action or process begins that is at once specific and different for each person. In order that it continue to be renewed, we normally practise the latihan twice a week. Each latihan lasts half an hour and takes place usually with a group, but when it is established in a person it can be practised alone in addition to the group latihans. Some people, especially those who are very self-conscious and find it hard to quieten the mind, can take a long time to 'receive', that is, to feel spontaneous movements or vibrations. Men and women never do it in the same room, for in the state of openness sexual attraction might arise, and this is out of place in the privacy of our relation to the power of God.

The mystery of simplicity

A friend who is a Greek Orthodox theologian once asked me for the actual meaning of the word 'latihan'. I told him it meant 'training' or 'exercise'. 'Then it's exactly the same as the Greek word "askesis",' he said, 'But,' I replied, 'it means an action not by us but by God within us.' 'So does "askesis".' We were both surprised. He explained that the words 'ascetic' and 'asceticism' and the severe abstinence they implied were a debasement of the original meaning. One had to be self-disciplined of course, and attentive; only then could the grace of God enter with its clarifying power.

Even now, how much has been said might explain the inward thing that happens at an 'opening' and in the latihan?

It is told that during the early persecutions of the Christians a Roman citizen was brought before the magistrates. How, he was asked, could an intelligent man like him, with all the time-honoured pantheon of the ancient gods to hold on to, be impressed by the rituals of a despised, mainly lower class sect? He could not explain or describe how he was moved in the depth of his being when he shared with quiet, humble people a holy meal of bread and wine in memory of a risen saviour, and what proceeded from this. He answered in two words: *mysterium simplicitatis*.

When the Roman spoke of the 'mystery of simplicity', he was clearly referring to Christian 'grace' which is – as I understand it – equivalent to what Bapak continually referred to as the *hakekat*. This is the 'inner content' or 'reality' of all true religion, the proof of something real that we come to be given through the sincere practice of the latihan. It is to be distinguished from the *shariat*, or outer form of observances and moral teaching. There is sometimes a confusion here because Bapak tended to speak only of the latter as religion, whereas for Christians both are included in the term. But the distinction between *hakekat* and *shariat* is basic and will be referred to later in this book.

Subud and Islam

The fact that Bapak was a Muslim has given the great majority of us who are not Muslims a sympathetic feeling towards Islam which we would hardly otherwise have reached. Simply being with Muslims time and again as we practise the latihan has the effect of rinsing away age-old prejudices, and the effect of hostile images of Islam dwelt on in the western media.

Another link has been fasting. A large number of non-Muslims among us have taken part regularly, or for some years, in the annual Ramadhan fast, attempting to follow it the way Bapak often spoke of, with emphasis on inner watchfulness as much as on outer restraint (see page 60). After all, through the ages fasting as a means of inner discipline, cleansing and renewal has been a normal part of religious practice, and Subud is only bringing back, along with some other movements in the church, what has become of value. For my own part, the times of following Ramadhan were an education in the meaning of and the need to practise Lent, which Bapak has said has equal high value with the Muslim fast.

Bapak himself never sought to make converts to Islam, which would have been totally against the spirit of Subud. But, being himself a supreme exemplar of the breadth and depth of Islam, he could not help exerting an influence. Not a few westerners

15

among us, having no roots or education in religion or being put off by the Judaism or Christianity they were brought up with, have embraced Islam, at least as a stage in their religious journey. Some of these converts, it must be said, having received a Muslim name and joined Islam in an elevated state, have found it difficult to follow the requirements of a faith outside their own culture and so have fallen away and reverted to their original names.

But how do those who are firm in Islam, it is asked – and they also ask themselves – stand in relation to the conservative and authoritarian forces which are at present sweeping through Islam on the one hand, and the modernising and westernising tendencies which oppose them on the other?

Those who write in 'Evidences' answer this question in a variety of ways. The Islam to which they bear witness is very different from the popular image prevailing in the West. The issue of human authority is avoided because the practice of the latihan enables them to experience the pure source of authority beyond man. One Algerian-born Muslim who is also a psychologist suggests that Subud, being outside these conflicts, offers a new model, or paradigm, of change, through which the present divisions might in time be made obsolete.

Bapak and Christianity

Nothing about Bapak has moved me as much as his deep familiarity with my own faith. It was not that Bapak grew up in a society in which Christian missionaries were respected, or at least tolerated, and that when young he had close friends who were Catholics, nor that as a Muslim much of Jewish and Christian scripture was part of his own inheritance. It was far beyond this. Bapak spoke of Jesus more often than of Muhammad and when he did it was often with a freshness and intimacy and considerable inner knowledge, which to a Christian can be both unnerving and revelatory.

In his earliest talks Bapak would refer in the usual Muslim way to *nabi*, or prophet, Jesus. After a little while in the West he dropped this and, while using *nabi* for Abraham, Moses and Muhammad, always said simply Jesus or Jesus Christ. On one occasion he spoke of the Light that came down into Jesus when he was born and remained with him as a child, adding that this Light was only visible to a few. At once something in me responded: but of course that must have been so! The mystery of the Christmas story suddenly was clarified. Only those who were clear and clean enough in themselves, such as the shepherds on the hillside and the three wise men, could be aware of a glow above and around Jesus. Had I been there, as an intellectual, I certainly would not have seen the light.

When Bapak alluded to Jesus feeding the multitude, the walking on the water or healing of sick and raising the dead, he would give these stories both a deep inner meaning and a psychological content: 'To walk on the water means to overcome and purify human emotions'.

'Be simple like children in order to receive the Truth,' Bapak would say, echoing the words of Jesus that we must be like little children if we are to enter the Kingdom of Heaven. On the physical plane spontaneous movements in the latihan are, indeed, often like those of helpless babies or young children playing, for most of us start at that stage in the development of our inner selves.

Most striking of all is when Bapak spoke of Jesus and of the manner of his death. He points up the fact and reality of the crucifixion and empathises with the suffering on the cross in a way perhaps unprecedented for a Muslim (see page 57).

Among those who sent in contributions to this book (not all printed here) no fewer than ten Subud members tell of an occasion when they were suddenly aware, in their feelings or visually, of Jesus being near to them or of the presence of Mary beside them. One member, going through a critical moment in his life, describes how he was in his bedroom and was spontaneously brought to his knees in latihan, aware only of a great light.

> I sat back on my heels, eyes tight shut but as though open wide. The light dazzled and took the form of some immeasurable mighty presence that towered above me through the roof and into the night sky above. I touched the floor with my forehead, then came a dawning, an unbearable realisation, that I was at the feet of Jesus, there in front of me and within touch. I passed out. When later I told Bapak something of what had taken place, he said, 'You see Jesus when you are truly repentant.'[4]

How can a Christian not feel awe for a Muslim from whom such personal words could come? Yet Bapak never wished us to feel awe towards himself, but only towards the power and source of his mission in the world. Only God may be called great.

Bapak and the Quakers

Bapak was once asked a question to do with the Quakers (by the present editor, through a third party). He said at once, 'But George Fox – he was opened!' That he should be aware of the spiritual stature of the founder of the Society of Friends is perhaps not surprising. More remarkably, Bapak went on to say that in his day George Fox and his friends received what we do in the latihan, with vibrations and movements, but were unable to pass the same spontaneity of receiving on to the next generation. By the third generation it was decided that worship beginning in silent communion was their way. Indeed, Quakers themselves sometimes wonder what was the reason for the quick decline of early power and fervour into the quietism of the eighteenth century which belied the derogatory nickname they adopted. But how could Bapak speak with apparent knowledge about a matter obscure to those most concerned? Not from being aware, as he said now and then, that Quakers were a good model for humanitarian action.

People, indeed, sometimes find it helpful to explain Subud by saying, 'It is rather like the Quakers.' There are clear differences but striking parallels. 'Be still awhile from thine own thoughts, desires and imaginings, and be stayed in the principle of God in thee up to God.' This advice of George Fox could be a preparation for the practice of the latihan. The doctrine of the 'inner light', the waiting in silence, the absence of dogma, the answering to 'that of God in everyone', the idea of a 'secret power' and that each meeting for worship is an 'experiment', that is, arising out of experience: all these are, to some extent, paralleled in Subud (see also page 84).

The need to practise one's religion

In the last year of his life Bapak spoke more definitely than before about the need to practise a religion, giving two main reasons. If we think that attendance at latihan is enough, he said, this will lead to a feeling of separateness from our fellow men and women. It will also lead to 'a decline in the state of our souls' (see page 67). Many of those who have found the latihan and the deep fellowship of Subud with, perhaps, a personal closeness to Bapak during his lifetime to be all in all may find this a hard saying. But I wonder if Bapak was not telling the great majority of us to be more in touch with the religious wisdom of the ages, and the whole wide realm of prayer.

At the same time, there are those who have sincerely wished to embrace or return to, say, Christianity but, when they go to church, find the services alien, or bland and routine. They seek in vain a minister or a congregation with whom they can feel comfortable. A few, on going to church, have even found themselves stigmatised as belonging to a cult and have been made to feel unwanted. Many of us, too, who never attend a place of worship are content to express their religious feeling of oneness with humanity by being active in the social field, and in regular private prayer.

'Coming home' to religion

Those who write below in 'Evidences' often tell how they have 'come home' to their own religion; how it is as real to them as is their mother; how they have arrived at last 'in their right place', perhaps far from where they started; how there is a falling away of doctrinal problems and divergence with those who worship differently.

If members feel 'in their right place', unbothered at all by what others believe, does this mean, then, that there can be no place for theology in Subud? Why not let the inner experience, the *hakekat* or Grace of God, be what unites humanity and say no more? Indeed, people are often drawn to Subud because in Subud there are no doctrines or dogmas to be accepted, no creed or 'rules'. Have not these been the cause of bitter divisions, fanaticism and wars? Is theology, say some of us, any more than an enticing but ultimately unproductive activity of the mind?

At the end of this book an American doctor of theology, herself a Christian but also a teacher of Islam, gives the opposite point of view as part of her 'evidence': that Subud from its very nature presents theological perspectives to the world and that, if we do not examine them ourselves, others will do so for us, and not always favourably. However, she adds, to enter into controversy is fruitless, for Subud offers an experience which transcends the truth claims of different religions. Her approach, which she calls a 'holy tentativeness' is a way of facing what is ultimately beyond explanation.

One humanity

During one Subud World Congress, held in Tokyo, I found myself lying in a steaming communal bath – that happy feature of Japanese life. All I could see at eye-level all around me were apparently decapitated male heads from every continent: a narrow-eyed, bald Malaysian, a red-haired Scot, a full-lipped fuzzy African, a man from Surinam with high narrow forehead and more still. Joined by our common latihan as much as by the ruffled water, they were my brothers, though I did not know them personally. There was the strange joy of accumulating riches. How superb to belong to the human race, to be linked with its infinite variety! How far off was the arrogant racist Englishman of my upbringing!

But why only my Subud brothers? The next day I was in a scorching Tokyo street, one foot on a box beneath me a skinny, wrinkled crone, half in rags but mistress of her craft. She was cleaning my shoes, going through several stages as she established a base on which to put the lacquer finish. She talked at me in a lively, laughing, toothless lingo, occasionally looking up. I nodded and smiled, tuned into the life-force which joined us; difference had fallen away. We had recognised each other in our humanity. Paying her I walked away but kept glancing back, reluctant to unhook my eyes from someone who a moment before had seemed to exist at the opposite pole to my own being and nature. Others tell similar stories of sudden complete conjunction with a total stranger.

Next day in the Congress, Bapak gave a definition of Subud as all humanity under the grace of God. So our name has no limit to its meaning. Bapak also once said, speaking about the development of real culture: What God loves is your own nature and not what you imitate. So, if you develop your own (true) national characteristics, you will be closer to God and the result will be no hatred of one nationality for another.[5]

The latihan as cleansing

A Quaker friend, once treasurer of a Friends Meeting in Surrey, used to go to the committee room once a month to present his accounts. There was always a 'weird noise' coming through the wall. What's that? he asked. Oh, that's Subud. They come here every week. What are they doing? They don't tell us, but they seem normal decent people.

For a few this sound is the first evidence that Subud exists. For the latihan, or training of the inner self, is also an act of clearing and cleansing, of throwing off, each person acting according to his nature and condition. We are enabled gradually to get rid of the results of both our own wrong-doing and that inherited from our forbears. Two lines of W.B. Yeats wonderfully describe for me the process:

> Nor can there be work as great
> As that which cleans man's dirty slate.

Being a rather physical person with a trusting nature, forceful movements came to me very soon, and I was noisy too. Quite a few like me at Coombe Springs were put in a group alone, so as not to disturb the others. I was proud of being singled out, imagining these strong reactions, or 'abreactions', were a sign of rapid progress, rather than perhaps of my physicality, excitement, or the dirtiness of my slate. I should add that the 'noise' made by the women in latihan can be extremely beautiful, even angelic-sounding, and that by men harmonious and richly polyphonic.

Approximately 100,000 people are said to have been opened in Subud and perhaps a tenth of that number have stayed and still practise the latihan. We gather to do so in our homes, in our own Subud houses, or in hired halls (in England quite often Quaker Meeting Houses); in converted cow sheds and garages and in deconsecrated churches; in quiet offices after hours, with the desks pushed back; under domes; in the cramped living rooms of eastern Europe (keeping the sound low); in straw-roofed huts in equatorial Africa; silently in or beside a hospital bed; in a prison cell. In all of these places the latihan is being followed humbly, gratefully, faithfully, indispensibly, joyfully, hopefully, sporadically, out of habit or out of inner necessity for the refreshment it often brings. But time and place are not necessary. The quiet presence of the latihan may be experienced spontaneously and privately at any moment.

At big international meetings I have been in a great latihan for many hundreds together. These are special, astonishing occasions. 'Relax' – a short pause – 'begin' says a helper. There is a huge spontaneous burst of sound, a rise and fall of voices in the minor key, chantlike, building up a drone; cries to God, to Allah, praising, praying; near me someone is sobbing, another mouthing strange words; people are dancing, running, spinning, waving their arms, contorting their bodies, but avoiding and ignoring each other; someone is kneeling, holding his head, another lying curled on the ground; others are stock-still and at peace. No one is in a trance and everyone feels normal and fully conscious of what is happening to and around them.

Gradually the chanting becomes more harmonious and movements tail off into a deep hush or else the helper has to call out through the noise, 'finish'. We are all cleaner, calmer inside, peaceful, closer together. We have been worshipping God. Strange but real! Next morning, perhaps, I am at a Quaker Meeting, or Holy Communion. All three for me belong together.

Do I say too much, or too little? What, you may ask, is the use of something so palpably absurd? What good has the latihan done you? Does it change people lastingly? What has Subud to show for itself? What are its fruits in the world? These are the right questions. Bapak frequently asked the same questions. It is up to us, the members, to prove that Subud works and is good.

Testing in Subud

Several reference and other books refer to 'testing' as a special feature of Subud. The word, now used by Subud members in all languages and confusing even to ourselves, is in fact a mistranslation from the Indonesian *terima*, or 'receive'. It is like a 'sixth sense' which can become more acute through the latihan and which, with practice, and the quietening of the other senses, we can call upon in need. Since it begins with asking for guidance and then surrendering one's own ideas and wishes, it has a certain kinship with petitionary prayer.

It was typical of Bapak that he should have once preceded a testing session with members by speaking poetically about the nature of birds who 'possess instincts which are like the taste of divine decrees'.[6] If they live on the slopes of a volcano about to erupt, they fly away in good time to safety. If bird-catchers approach the trees where they congregate, they likewise disappear. If birds can feel like that, Bapak went on, why can't human beings who possess a far finer set of equipment have correspondingly acute feelings? He then proceeded to show those present how they could, through testing, experience in themselves the nature and condition of another person – a tangible way of being, in St. Paul's phrase, 'members of one another'. The wider meaning of the Russian orthodox word *sobornost*, the inner connectedness of the self with other selves, is full of significance for us, just as lovers in their open state to each other 'know' that there can – and must – be a connectedness across space. Telepathy is frequently vouched for. That North American Indians, like Kalahari and Australian bushmen, can know or send messages at a distance holds little surprise for most Subud members.

We acknowledge telephathy in several ways, as with latihans simultaneously co-ordinated between, say, a group and an isolated or sick member, or in a world latihan which takes place usually once a month, synchronously during the same half hour all over the world for those who wish.

This brings to mind the Marshall McLuhan concept of the 'global village'. This famous phrase for the results of instantaneous electronic communication across the world can be seen as a paradigm of Subud, but at the material level – the level of thought. In the Subud mode there is also a banishment of distance. But the wave-bands, so to speak, are not packed with information and images, with opinion and argument. Rather, the channels are clean and open for quiet inner feeling to reach out and receive; the intimation of instantaneous linkage is yet another confirmation of the oneness of humanity.

'Testing' or 'receiving' implies that in seeking the way to right living there is a source of guidance and instruction cleaner and stronger than our usual desires and thoughts. To be able to test according to need is one of the most valuable gifts offered by

Subud, an aid to the task of right living. Through it we can be shown how to act or behave in circumstances where we are in deep doubt and difficulty.

This is not the place to describe the actual procedures of a testing 'session'. It suffices to say that, rather as in petitionary prayer, guidance is asked for by the person involved, supported by a few helpers, all being quietly in the latihan state. To give two examples; a man has reached an impasse in his work – what should he do about it? Or a wife is being badly treated by her husband – how can she change the situation? The answers to questions (discussed and agreed beforehand) may be received in body-language (such as a movement meaning 'yes' or 'no', or a gesture which shows the right attitude to have) or in a few words of insight and/or a flood of inner feeling.

Those who ask may receive nothing, meaning 'no action' or that there is a deeper question to be put: it may be that the man's problem at work is in his own nature, or that he is in the wrong work and should change it. The right course for the wife might be to be truly patient with her husband, or the opposite: to confront him for the first time with her actual feelings towards him. In both cases a clear course of action is indicated, and the important thing is that the person concerned should 'receive' for himself or herself.

We may think of testing as a direct guidance from God, as a group form of personal petitionary prayer, or as enhanced intuition mutually arrived at. If we treat testing lightly, or do it without real need, or don't follow the guidance received, we lower its value and blunt its acuity. If we test too much we can weaken our will and our power to make decisions and take responsibility for them.

Above all, it should be stressed that there is nothing occult about testing. It is neither an oracle nor divination. Testing increases trust and openness between members, as we gradually become more transparent to each other. Much of this breaking down of falsity is what also happens in ordinary counselling and therapy sessions. In Subud, too, natural or trained skills in listening draw out the truth of a situation and discover the important question to ask which might be hidden behind the original one. A caring attentiveness may so clarify the problem that the answer is clear and no question needs to be asked.

New eyes and the vanity of riches

When I first came into Subud I told a wise man who was counselling me at the time about my wonderful discovery. He said smiling, but with a note of warning, 'It sounds exciting.' It was, and soon became more so – not only those powerful throwing-off latihans and the strange newness of testing but moments of sudden insight, as when I heard or read familiar passages of the Bible with new ears, new eyes.

Once I was cleaning up my workshop, itself a symbolic act, when I looked through the window across a field. Something seemingly vaporous was descending on the grass, as though it were dew. But it could not be dew for it was a clear summer day. It was a physical vision of grace descending. 'I must write and tell so-and-so,' it came to me, 'he'll be impressed.' At once the vision was cut off as by a switch. I censored the self-admiring thought, and immediately the air above the field was alive again, though only for a short while. I believe I was being shown that the gift of grace was always showering down on us did we but know. The vision has never come again.

At another time in a waking dream I was descending a mountain by a deep gully piled high with big boulders. I kicked one of the boulders. It was so light that it bounded out of the way as though it had been a giant ping-pong ball. I did this all the way down the gully, clearing a path. It was a very Christian image. When I told a French Benedictine monk in Subud (see page 131) he wrote back, 'Your rocks signify a certain situation. Thanks to the latihan, obstacles interior and exterior fly away. But you need courage to confront them. If you look at them from afar they appear like mountains, but with the help of God we have this faculty that can remove mountains. 'Say unto that mountain, be removed into the sea, and it will be removed' (St. Luke 4; St. Matthew 22).'

From such insights I convinced myself that I was making spiritual progress. Subud was a great adventure, and I was good at it. It was taking me to inner places and heights and understandings of which I had never dreamed. My ego was distinctly flattered.

The coming of Subud might, as in the book of that name, be an 'antidote' to the ills of the world. In my case antidotes were needed to my vanity. One was administered during a service in the Cathedral of Cefalu in Sicily on a Palm Sunday. In the dome is a huge Byzantine mosaic, one of the greatest of all Christ Pantocrators, at once awesome and benevolent. Under his all-seeing eye I was caught up in the traditional devotion and drama of the service, and felt at one with the great throng of worshippers. Although not a Catholic, I was pushed from within to go up and receive the sacrament. Waiting in the queue I was suddenly aware of myself as a nobody, as utterly ordinary, like a pebble on the beach, not different from all the others, from millions. It was a strangely welcome sensation and high time. I had allowed myself to feel special and different as a Subud member for far too long. It is less rare now for me to catch my ego on a self-admiring jaunt and to say to it, 'Just you shut up!'

A sense of being this same pebble comes to me sometimes when in the latihan I am brought to my knees with head and arms huddled on the floor, as small as can be. Above me I hear rising and falling the chanting voices of my brothers washing over me in a cleansing motion as I lie as if on the bottom of a river. It may not look like it from my outer behaviour, but I never feel more gratefully and authentically a member of Subud than at such moments.

A rabbi's image for Subud

The numerous published experiences of Subud members are full of signs and wonders and the unexpected, as early proofs of a new reality. Bapak once said, 'From the start, the instant of opening, you receive from God "the whole package" as it were.'[7] Without climbing we may be lifted high enough to see the possibilities that lie ahead, a view beyond the ridge of doubt. But a long hard journey may lie ahead, a descent into rocky or swampy valleys where the going is rough, and there is only a memory of that distant vista.

A perceptive rabbi once told a Subud member that there are two ways to come into full possession of a spiritual home. In one you work hard, save and bank the money and after so long you can walk into the house. In the other you obtain a mortgage and live in your house at once; but if you don't keep up the regular payments the house will be taken from you. The second way, this rabbi suggested, is Subud. The payments must go on and on – the pain of growth, giving up the pride and imaginings of your ego – or you are on the street again.

'You are pioneers'

Bapak often spoke of Subud members as pioneers. He was the bringer of the latihan, this unexpected gift, fresh into the world. We were not his followers, but co-workers, learning under his guidance to find our own individual inner guidance. Only through us could Bapak discover what Subud in action could achieve.

At the beginning in the West the emphasis was on the spiritual, on the deepening and stabilising of the latihan experience. After a decade Bapak was encouraging us to prove its worth in the turmoil of the world. But his vision of God and working for ourselves and our families and the good of all humanity went together. At the first World Congress in 1959, human welfare was the theme that attracted most interest. By the beginning of that year a Subud Human Welfare Trust had already been founded, which nine years later became the Subud Brotherhood International Foundation, registered in Geneva. (In 1989 it became known as the Subud Association International Foundation.) The vision was that Subud would become known through what its members did for the poor and sick, for refugees, for the disabled and the handicapped, the old and the illiterate; there would be Subud hospitals and schools and we ourselves would provide the finance for these.

As a youth Bapak had admired the commercial skill and energy of the Dutch in developing the material resources of his own country. All the more when he came to the West, he could see the potential of western capitalism to create wealth and prosperity which would be for all. Unlike most oriental sages (and some western thinkers) Bapak was not antagonistic to modern science and the progress of technology – even though it had enabled man in his passions to 'become more dangerous than the tiger'. It was a proper field for the thinking mind of man and had huge possibilities for still further development. It was for the use of humanity, only it must be under the direction not of those who were fascinated and dominated by material forces, but of those possessing the true qualities of a human being (Susila).

The spiritual dimension of work

Around 1970 the word 'enterprise' was more and more on Bapak's lips – in English. He would pronounce it slowly with three equally emphasised syllables and gave it, like 'latihan', an extra dimension of meaning. En-ter-prise was to stand on one's own feet and not be a wage-slave, to discover one's talent and use it, to be energetic and resourceful, to support one's family and give a portion to charity. This last is a spiritual duty and the principle of the Fourth Pillar of Islam – the *zakat*.

Bapak left us another spiritual-psychological reason for 'enterprises'. This is in order to combat the ancient idea that the search for inner knowledge is incompatible with work (see page 53). Holding to this was 'to go back into the cave'. Enterprises are a way of forcing us to be part of the everyday world we live in with all its frictions and competition, and not allow the good and perhaps high feelings we may receive through the latihan to tempt us, as they have sometimes tempted me, to escape from it. I think of former hippies guided by the latihan to take on big responsibilities, of those who hoped to avoid what they thought of as the rat race but have come back in and been successful, no longer feeling themselves in the least to be rats.

One day the Latin motto of my old school came alive for me: *orando laborando*. Literally it means, 'Through praying, through working.' I used to think it mediaeval, monastic and a bit odd. In a flash I saw how close it is to what Bapak was telling us: worship and work belong together, and reinforce each other because they can have the same content. It is doing that gives meaning to prayer, and prayer that gives content to action. I believe that all of us now and then can get a hint or taste of this when we are doing well and calmly the work that is right for us. We feel good inside, with extra energy and a lightness of being, and have a sense of being at one with the universe, as children do when they are busy and happy. Best of all is when this happens with several people working together.

In order to show that work as worship can be natural for anyone, Bapak would chuckle about the bank clerk counting notes, and all the while the same rhythm 'Allah, Allah, Allah' is going on inside him. At the opposite extreme, Bapak used to say; 'Do not think that God does not work. If God did not work, the world would vanish.'

Growing pains and Subud enterprises

Bapak himself set in motion several large enterprises, drawing on the financial, managerial and architectural skills of members across the world. Among them have been a fine latihan hall with the first pre-stressed concrete roof in Indonesia; a bank in which thousands of us had shares, housed in a striking office block in Jakarta and bearing Bapak's family name – Widjojo; a prestigious conference centre near Windsor, 'Anugraha'. Pride and expectations were generated by these and other undertakings and also a high level of investment from members – estimated at £32 million. The rest was found in bank loans. Since Bapak watched personally over these projects and the managers were practising the latihan, how could they not, we told ourselves, all succeed? Hoped-for profits would accrue and help finance our international organisation and the setting up of the human welfare projects that would make the name of Subud sweet in the world.

It did not happen that way. Loan burdens increased, share values fell and much investment, especially in some, larger projects, was wiped out. The Widjojo project is prospering but Anugraha, the conference centre, after a brilliant period, suffered from 'aspiration overrun' and was put in the hands of a receiver.

All this is now seen as part of the painful growing process of Subud, a testing and training in realities, and gave rise to a common saying among us: Subud is not a teaching, but it is a great learning.

There are signs at the time of writing that the Subud 'enterprise culture' is beginning to find its feet. No longer do members plunge into business without a talent for it. Going back to college, personal development and team building workshops are becoming more common. Numerous enterprises, both in the West and in developing countries, have survived and some have done very well, to the benefit of Subud social aims, ranging from a picture framing business to a Welsh outdoor management training centre, from health food stores and a successful hotel to a major laser manufacturer.

A much fuller treatment of work and enterprises can be found in Dominic Rieu's *A Life Within A Life* (pages 155–78).

Susila Dharma and human welfare

The World Subud Council has formed so-called 'wings' for enterprises, cultural activities and youth (sometimes combined) and human welfare. The last of these is at present the most active. When those two Sanscrit words, Susila Dharma, which are contained within the word 'Subud' were first given as the name of the human welfare wing of Subud, there were those who feared it might be a handicap as it conveys nothing to a western public and might even appear odd. But Bapak gave the name and, in his wisdom, persisted with it.

For a long time Susila Dharma International (SDI) was for me simply the Subud charity, worthy of special support because it was ours. It was not much different from giving to a doorstep appeal or covenanting to Oxfam: I was doing my social duty, minutely lessening the inequality of the world, showing up as a caring person. Since working more actively with Susila Dharma I've come to understand that these words demand more of me than this. If *susila* is active inside me I will be aware both of my own worth and dignity as a human being and also of the same in my fellow beings, and because of this empathy I will also know their condition and needs. *Dharma*, which means trust, sincerity and submission of my own self-will, provides the impulse to act on this.

This brings me, as a Christian, very close to those challenging words which Jesus singled out from the Hebrew Book of Leviticus and made one of the two great universal commandments: Thou shalt love thy neighbour as thyself. Bapak in one of his pregnant sayings put it this way: social work is a sign of the link between one soul and another.

The same can be also expressed in non-moral and non-religious language. Helping others is not then a matter of 'should' or 'ought' inculcated by parents or education, by peer group or public opinion. Nor is it the carrying of a social burden which implies inequality and distance between people. A German SDI trustee puts it like this: 'There is something in each of us which responds automatically to another's need if we allow it to do so. It is a very simple mechanism that does not require any educational appeal.'

A passage from *The Meditations of Marcus Aurelius* fits here perfectly:

What more do you want when you have done a man a service? Are you not content that you have done something conformable to your nature? And do you seek to be paid for it, just as if the eye demanded a reward for seeing and the feet for walking?

The famous and virtuous Roman Emperor was a Stoic philosopher and humanist and did not have to believe in God to write this.

Susila Dharma International, the international organisation at present located in Britain, does not itself initiate projects, but exists with a small office at the service of Susila Dharma representatives and committees in thirty-six of the countries where Subud has taken root. Its task is to nourish and inspire local initiatives and to foster the innate caring abilities and commitment of members. Fundraising takes place both at the centre and locally.

Since 1982 forty-eight newsletters (now a quarterly magazine, *Outlook*) have described the building up of health care and schooling in slums and shanty towns in the developing world, and among refugee children in Europe; homes or refuges for the handicapped, the aging, the deprived, the neglected and abused; places where youth can learn skills and hope. When two Norwegian professors (with an Israeli professor not in Subud) develop child development programmes for the disadvantaged now being used in seven countries; when care is being pioneered for the neglected old (because the family system is breaking down), or a rigid school system is injected with progressive, holistic ideas of education; when black students repay a bursary so that others can follow them to college; when in six years a pre-school in a slum grows into a community and vocational training centre for a whole neighbourhood; when a personal rescuing of orphaned street children leads on to a children's village; when one man in gratitude to God sends four million dollars worth of medical supplies from out-dated stock to poor countries; when all this is achieved it may still be an insignificant contribution to healing the ills of the world, but very important for us in Subud as evidence of what we call 'the latihan at work'.

In all this, support from several well-known development agencies and foundations has been crucial, but the SDI policy is that Subud people should be responsible for the content of such projects, the spirit in which they develop. Susila Dharma is dedicated to bridging the psychological gap between the haves and the have-nots, between those who give and those who receive assistance, no matter what faith or culture they belong to. This is

31

because of the common inner feeling that already exists between those who do the latihan, between the donors in richer countries and, say, Sri Lankans and Colombians who have responded to the crying needs in their own countries.

Indeed, this common feeling is natural between all who work within the Susila Dharma framework, whether as fundraisers or trustees, as administrators and secretaries and committee members, as team leaders and workers, or those who write about it all. This helps the many project partnerships set up to be genuine at a time when this word is much abused, for instance, by government and bureaucratic bodies in order to flatter an economically weaker partner.

Since 1989 SDI has been affiliated to ECOSOC, the social arm of the United Nations, with consultative status. This provides another channel for Subud to become involved in big world issues such as refugees, world poverty, the needs of children and the environment. But, it should be clear, the words Susila Dharma are wider than this, for they cover all spontaneous acts of selfless human aid, whether set up in a formal way or simply as caring for one's neighbour.

Social democracy

During the thirty years of Bapak's mission to the world his vision of a possible future for Subud and for human society unfolded steadily and took on a clearer shape. In the seventies he began to speak of democracy and gave that tired and abused word a fresh, deceptively simple and clean meaning. It did not arise out of ideas of liberty, or human rights or equality, but from a deep-down sense of awareness of the shared humanity of all people. 'Democracy,' Bapak once said, 'is common feeling.' Some of us have seen this as one of his seminal remarks that predicates a whole new way of looking at politics.

When about the same time Bapak added the word 'social', it had not the least connection with political doctrine. Social democracy is about how humans behave towards each other. It exists 'wherever there is a true morality, where money is never used to harm others and people know how to divide their funds – so much for this and that, so much for oneself, so much for others.' Such qualities cannot develop where there are gross inequalities, but only when everyone has at least a 'sufficiency to meet their needs'. A simple example of social democracy in action is 'the feeling of oneness when people gather for a birth or a funeral'.

Such guidance about behaviour is very necessary for Subud members, especially when they are working on committees, which play an important part in the inner as well as the outer growth of Subud. Bapak used to pronounce the word *ko-mi-té* emphatically with a precise gesture of the fingers, as if to say, 'Don't you understand? I am offering you something important, a tool you really need in order to progress.' Committees can of course be boring, but not when we use them to deal with realities and they become exercises in honesty. In committees and workshops we can come to understand and appreciate one another better, valuing the strengths of each and accepting their weaknesses. Moreover since, as has been explained, the way of the latihan is not only an inner training but a cleansing, our personal rubbish can then more easily come to the surface and be dissolved. Some of us have found that this process is helped by the current techniques of psychological group-work and team building.

If democracy is indeed 'common feeling', and we can really reach this state among ourselves, many things become possible. Susila and compassion have an easier field to work in. People are more frank and trusting with each other and initial quarrels are seen to have been 'useful friction'. Another person's worth and ability is acknowledged without envy, indeed gladly because it is for the benefit of everyone. Status become irrelevant and previous hierachical systems are simply unnecessary. A horizontal model takes its place, but not where everyone is evened out. On the contrary, human differences are cultivated, because people feel more free to act according to the creative energy, the *budhi*, of their own nature. In such a pluralistic, tolerant society people think more in terms of responsibility than rights, and responsibility itself is exercised as a service to the community, and never as power. The old sacred values, the commandments of God to man over the ages remain.

If there is something good and useful here for humanity in general, it is not for us in Subud to preach it, but rather to prove by working it out first among ourselves.

Bapak and Culture

Bapak saw culture as a way through which Subud could both develop and spread. At large gatherings and international conferences, especially when Bapak was himself present, music and dancing, stories and comic turns, art and craft exhibitions have been an essential feature, along with enterprise presentations and, latterly, creativity workshops. In Germany on two occasions the performances were delightful to the eye and had a good professional standard. Afterwards however, Bapak said it had been nice and what he was used to – but added, 'Isn't everything you are singing just imitation? – As with mynah birds' – who mimic what they hear.[8] It sounded crushing, but Bapak meant that the musicians and singers were *performing* in the way they had been taught, in the way they thought it ought to be done, and not from inner feeling.

Bapak was always happy when he found a member who could play with a clean inner feeling, without ego, or was on the verge of being able to do this. One such is the gifted violinist Maurice Isaacs who tells that when he played in Bapak's house in Bapak's presence a deep sense of freedom and lightness came over him. He connects this occasion with being at the annual Prad Festival with the great cellist Pablo Casals, 'After a while it was as though Casals, who played often, was not there personally. He became just like a prism through which the music of Bach reached directly into me. It was the most extraordinary two weeks of my life as a musician.'

When Dirk Campbell had the privilege of playing for Bapak at his wife Ibu Mastuti's birthday in July 1985 on the Irish 'uilleann' pipes, Bapak at first thought that this ancient Celtic music was not European music, which he knew as being more 'for the heart' than Asian music. He then went on to say that it is music which comes from an empty place inside one that actually has the power to reach other people. Dirk, Bapak said, was beginning to be able to play like this, but 'not yet from the deep inner'.

Bapak would tease us by saying that nowadays the birds did better than we did – when they sang it was spontaneously out of their own nature in praise of their maker while we made music not from our souls but for the entertainment of heart and mind, or to make money. 'For that reason culture, which used to be a living culture, is now a dead culture.'[9]

What did Bapak mean by speaking like this? It was, in fact, out of the roots of his own language that he invited us to look at the meaning of culture in an entirely fresh way. In Indonesian the term for culture or civilisation is *kebudayaan*, which is built up around *budhi*, the second of the trilogy of words contained in the name Subud. To *budhi* (see glossary) is added *daya*, which means 'power' or 'work'.

For Subud people *budhi* – the creative inner drive in each person – is demonstrated by the spontaneous movements we make in the latihan. It is from such an aliveness, Bapak says, that culture can arise, out of a person's individuality and skill, and stemming from their own innate and national characteristics. At Woodstock in 1977 he said, 'It is as if the latihan aims you in the direction of your own truth and reality, so that you will not imitate other people or their opinions.'[10] On that occasion Bapak defined culture very simply as 'the skill of the inner self.'

The second crucial factor for the presence of true culture is that it can only arise from a peaceful and calm feeling. It is born – like the major inventions – out of a quiet inner state. In the past it emerged from sacred places, from mosques, religious schools and Christian churches (see page 64). Culture arising from the calm of inner feeling, Bapak said at Anugraha in 1983, can point to the future and be a kind of symbol or indication of things before they happen. Through the peace and calm of inner feeling a person can know the right direction for human society, for their country and nation.

A year later Bapak, on listening to various reports, was surprised and pleased to learn that there are so many Subud people in the cultural field. It gave him the beginning, he said, of a picture of how Subud should develop: through acting or painting, through dancing or sculpture or other activities which possess real content and are themselves a way to God. And, because all this is what stems from the spiritual energy of the *budhi*, he included here social work as well and aspects of youth work.[11]

This is why SICA – the Subud International Cultural Association – has a central place with enterprises and welfare in the structure that Bapak left us.

It is not, however, for this book to try to show how far Subud members, either as artists on their own or combining together, have begun to give proof of what they receive in the latihan. But I sense that alongside us there are many creative spirits who, all too aware of the vacuity, mere nostalgia or honest despair in nearly all modern culture, have tapped into sources without ego, who are in touch with the sacred in the arts and are working for its renewal. Will they recognise, and perhaps feel, the place where Bapak's voice comes from?

This voice on occasions spoke in words which have an ancient, ageless simplicity that confounds an analysis, as when Bapak once received this spontaneous song (literally translated):

> In reality culture ought to be the expression of feeling
> A feeling that is pure and able to receive
> Affected and touched by the holy feeling known as the Holy Spirit
> The source of advice which is true.[12]

Those who are afraid of Subud

As might be expected, Subud is often seen as threatening to the established order, and not only under repressive regimes. In Eastern Europe, Subud had a clandestine existence for thirty years. The small group in East Berlin kept going in private houses. 'During this time,' a member tells, 'when we felt isolated and degraded by the very existence of the Wall, the latihan enabled us to maintain and develop our spiritual freedom.' In Czechoslovakia Subud was reported on by a disaffected member and 'investigated' by the security police. The severe restrictions then imposed had the effect of holding the small, aging group together, which owned a delightful secret Subud house deep in the Bohemian countryside. In Poland it is probable the S.B. were also well informed about Subud, but as the nation became less and less under the thumb of the Communist power, fear of oppression vanished. During the glasnost period in Russia several Muscovites were opened on visits to London.

Only in Cuba is the heavy hand of the state still felt by our members. The group was once infiltrated by the police. When it was imprudently decided to register Subud, which meant giving the names of office holders, they promptly lost their jobs. Totally cut off, members continued to meet for latihan, but without any news of the rest of Subud – except telepathically. During the month of June 1987 the core members for several days felt inexplicably heavy in spirit and had extremely strong latihans. Some time later they found it was just the time of Bapak's last illness and death.

In the eastern region of Malaysia it is officially forbidden for any Muslim to be a member of Subud. In Capetown active intolerance has grown lately and an *imam* has refused to marry a Muslim couple because they were Subud. In California Subud has been denounced on the radio and hostility has been shown in certain charismatic churches, where belonging to Subud has been regarded as peculiar and the member prayed for or asked to leave. In Christchurch, New Zealand, a woman minister visiting from England told the congregation that Subud was an evil religious cult, persuaded the then national chairman to renounce it publicly and took a number of assistants to exorcise his house.

Unaware that a Benedictine monk, Père Albert Bescond, and two fellow monks had been given permission by their Order to practise the latihan (see page 131), the Archbishop of Paris voiced his strong disapproval of any association with *ce culte quasi-Hindou*. In 1989 a newly opened Catholic member in London informed her Jesuit confessor who told her to desist from Subud as it was Islamic and prayed to Allah and not to the Trinity. Another Jesuit father in the same church entirely approves of Subud. Some nuns were opened in South America as a result of contact with Subud members and practised the latihan until their Mother Superior grew nervous of what higher authorities might say.

Joining Subud – and leaving

Subud is still an extremely small movement. The desired and nearly total absence of media attention has been a protection and a blessing, but must also be due to our small impact until now on the world at large. There are members thinly but unevenly spread in seventy countries, as many in Colombia as in the rest of South America, in Zaire as in the rest of Africa. There is a minimal organisation.

Local groups, which may have as few as two or three or as many hundreds of members, flourish, remain static or decline – points of light which blaze up, multiply, stay steady or flicker out. Subud does not evangelise. People join us through reading a book; through an encounter which seems 'meant'; by osmosis with friend, marriage partner or lover; through suddenly seeing or hearing the word Subud and recognising its power (though some are put off by it); through example and the evidence of observing someone change; by being born of Subud parents, though this by no means follows naturally.

Very few join Subud because someone hopes they will. Husbands are advised not to press wives to join, and vice-versa. My own wife came in prematurely because of my urging; it was several years before she re-joined of her own accord. Now and then, I've thought: I'll tell so-and-so about Subud – it might be what they need. Then I've watched them listening with no ears to hear and with their minds only. They were forming a fixed mental picture of Subud which could be an obstacle when it came their way again and when they might be more ready. So we tend to keep quiet, even with our friends, which can give the quite wrong impression that Subud is secretive.

Another obstacle is when a keen applicant has false expectations: joining Subud is going to be wonderful – they are such lovely people! This euphoric fantasy (which can also exist afterwards) hampers trust in the unexpected and the state of emptiness which is the condition for receiving the contact.

'Better not come into Subud', we sometimes warn, only half jokingly, 'your whole life might get turned upside down.'

People leave the Subud organization because the latihan has never really 'caught'; because they are not stayers and lose their early excitement; because helpers lecture them or ignore them and members are unfriendly; because, if they are young, they find no one like themselves and the older members seem crusty; because they leave no space inside themselves for change; because of quarrelling; because they take Subud for granted and do not pay the inner mortgage as in the Rabbi's story. One hears of some who seem to leave – they are on no list – but continue to practise the latihan on their own. Others join us and find the spark or quickening they were looking for, for example healing power, material success or religious vision, and then are seen no more.

Being close to Bapak

There is a new generation of Subud members who have never heard or seen Bapak in person. We who often sat at his feet cherish our memories of him. Aided by a journal, I can still see him in the old latihan hall at Cilandak in 1970. It is a late November evening during Ramadhan. Bapak sits cross-legged on a mat, wearing a flat Javanese turban. Under the folds of his sarong his bare feet appear as immaculate as his hands. On a low table beside him are sweetmeats, as beside all hundred and more of us, and coffee. The warm air holds a distinct spicy smell from the clove dust in the 'Bentul' cigarettes that Bapak and many of us are smoking. There is occasional backchat and laughter with the intimate circle of Indonesians as he mixes all the moods, commenting on life, receiving high things.

Bapak asks us to tell of experiences so far in Ramadhan. When someone claims a deep one Bapak says it is not deep, but in the imagination – the real ones will come towards the end of the fast. He speaks about the need to be in the right state in order to be able to help someone, giving the example of a father who has asked him why he has a bad relationship with his son (both are present). It's really the fault of the father, Bapak says, for trying to help the son directly. He proceeds into a little homily about the duty of parents not to interfere with the lives of their children once they are past eighteen. If we keep advising them about what to do, we enter into their private sphere where they are trying to work out their own future, and they are bound to reject the invasion. But since we are inwardly connected with our children, our prayers and even occasional fasting can help the 'inner' of the child to receive the help he or she needs. The basic message, which Sjarif Horthy sums up as a typical way of Bapak saying things, is: God wants to help people to live rightly, but if parents get too much in the way, He doesn't bother.

We sit for three and a half hours which speed by. At the end Bapak lifts the level to another plane by singing an ancient song in an ethereal voice.

In Europe Bapak always wore a smart suit and tie and on his head a black *peci*, filling the armchair with a commanding benevolent presence. On a low table between him and Sjarif would be a jug of Coca-cola. He would lean out towards us to communicate his urgency and a fatherly affection. His fascinating range of gestures with arms, hands and fingers was never in the least histrionic. Though I understood barely a word, just listening to the eager modulated flow of his baritone voice, which he often punctuated with an infectious chuckle, could be totally satisfying in itself. It might continue for twenty minutes or more, so great was Sjarif's power to internalise. The saying would come back to me of Papunahang, an enlightened Pennysylvanian Indian, when he had been listening to the preaching of the Quaker John Woolman, who had dispensed with an interpreter: 'I love to feel the place where the words come from.'

Sometimes Bapak would leave the chair for the front of the platform, to appear as a youngish man with a dancer's movements. He became a comedian, a mimic, the former Wayang clown, as he demonstrated, for instance, the influence on people of wearing expensive clothes, diamonds – or a revolver.

Bapak never spoke from behind a screen of spiritual omniscience. He could acknowledge he made mistakes, even asking our forgiveness for them.[13] He told us not to agree with everything he said, but to test it out in our lives. This for me was one of the early proofs that Bapak was authentic, and enabled me to put in a 'suspense account' things I could not agree with. A greater proof is the way I keep understanding more and more in his talks when I reread them or discover fresh ones.

Bapak, this one-time Javanese railwayman and book-keeper, illustrated his talks with wide-sweeping spiritual knowledge, historical allusions and contemporary references: to the difference between Socrates and Jesus;[14] to the hands of Rembrandt and the legs of the footballer Pele, when speaking about spontaneously developing talents;[15] to the sadness and anxiety of Christina Onassis, on the subject of 'wealth sickness' and how to avoid it.[16]

He told how he was aware when Russian and American nuclear submarines were stalking each other under the ocean round Java and of his pain when two Muslim countries, Iraq and Iran, fought during Ramadhan, and at the state of Beirut. He would get us to 'test' and feel these things for ourselves. In Hamburg in 1983 his listeners expressed fear of the consequences for their city of a nuclear war between Russia and America, which might be destroyed in ten minutes. Bapak calmed their anxiety and incredibly suggested another possible scenario in the future: the war might be between Russia and Russia. This was before Gorbachev and *glasnost* were heard of.[17]

Having written this far and unable to go on, I got up and walked to the window. It isn't good enough, I told myself. Suddenly I was laughing. There was no one in the house and I laughed on and on – at myself. It was, I suppose, a spontaneous 'test'. The message came like a gift and was quite clear: Do you really think you can get close to Bapak in those carefully arranged sentences? Aren't you trying too hard – being a bit heavy about it?

Bapak was fond of laughter and encouraged it in us. When someone is laughing the thinking mind is shut off. Laughter rinses away former thoughts when they are strained or worried or angry. My laughing at that moment released me from where I was into a great space beyond it. It put me, I believe, 'somehow' in touch with Bapak himself, with his spirit, with his lightness of being. Let it be, he was telling me. What you write isn't so important.

Laughter can clear the way through the unknown. Men visitors to Cilandak liked calling on Sudarto Martohujojo, who was one of Bapak's first helpers, a delightful and wise person who could see right inside one. Talk with him was always light and instructive and lifted with laughter. I once told him about my older brother, Ben, a great enjoyer of life and one of its victims, and how I had felt very close to him in his last despairing years. When he committed suicide I was horrified. Two days later I had a clear experience of the moment when Ben's spirit suddenly left his body for a far-off place. 'It was near at one moment and at the next incredibly distant. Where did he go to?' I asked.

The answer came: 'Because you were laughing just now when we spoke of him, you can reach him.'

I could not speak. I got up, embraced Mas Darto in his little room and walked away with tears of amazement and gratitude in my eyes.

Bapak once said, 'Laughter in the latihan means saying thank you to God.'[18] It was that sudden arrival of laughter and lightness at Coombe Springs in 1957 which had especially marked the change from the old regime to the new spirit of the place.

Bapak's Death and After

Following his last visit to England in 1986 Bapak moved to a new house at Pamulang in the country just outside Jakarta. That winter we heard he was very weak and living mostly in a world beyond this. But his strength kept returning and in the last days of May and Ramadhan he gave three brief talks. The word 'courage' occurred again and again. If Subud had not yet developed far it was because we lacked the courage to use what we had received.

By the time of his birthday celebrations on 22 June, to which numerous members came from overseas, Bapak was seriously ill with pneumonia. He rose from his bed and on the inside balcony of his house cut the top off the rice mountain (equivalent of a birthday cake) and stood while members sang Happy Birthday. In the throng looking up from below there was a feeling of 'inexpressible sadness suffused with gratitude and some deeper joy and awe'.[19] He raised his arms in frail farewell. *Sudah?* (Already over?), he asked and repeated as if in answer, *Sudah*. (Finished.)

That night Bapak talked a good deal to those around him 'in order to breathe better'. He spoke about the inevitable conflict between the spiritual and the material, of the need to be diligent in the latihan if Subud was to grow and of the need to show proof of the latihan in daily life. He spoke of our financial weakness and gave the last of innumerable definitions of Subud. It was (as reported) 'a spiritual reality or movement whose basis is social feeling – a feeling of wanting to help others, of loving others, of living aright and doing good.'

During the night Bapak's hold on life suddenly lessened and he was taken to hospital. He died en route, just before dawn on 23 June. His body was brought back to Pamulang and those who had attended his birthday, and many more, crowded back to pay their final homage. The funeral was on the same day. A cortege a mile long crossed Jakarta in the rain to the Karet cemetery. Here the last rites were performed and farewell speeches made, remembering that for a large part of this century Bapak had become a 'window through which God's grace came into the world, a world in which this is very much lacking.'

A round-the-clock vigil was kept at the tomb for forty days and nights, during which there were continuous readings from the Koran. It can be said too that the birds, which, in Bapak's words, 'possess instincts which are like the taste of divine decrees' (see page 23), also participated. A group of grave-diggers and attenders told how, some hours before Bapak breathed his last, great flocks of birds, some never before seen in the cemetery, arrived and settled in the trees round the Sumohadiwidjojo family graves. 'Then we knew that someone of great importance had died.'

On the third, seventh and hundredth days after Bapak's passing there took place in many centres across the world, following the Muslim custom, gatherings to give thanks and praise for his life.

In England, at the Anugraha Conference Centre, it was conducted on each occasion jointly by Subud brothers according to Jewish, Christian and Islamic rites. An Anglican minister included a Buddhist prayer, and each time the *imam* intoned the *zikr* many non-Muslims too found themselves swaying to its rhythms. We took this mutual embrace of the three religions for granted, although it is doubtful that any man had ever before been honoured in quite this way. Wide celebrations were also held on the thousandth day after Bapak's death, sixteen hundred members from all the continents gathering at the house in Pamulang.

The news of Bapak's death was momentous but it struck us prepared. It was known there would be no crisis of succession, no 'power vacuum', and that no member of Bapak's own family wished to inherit his mantle. We look to Bapak's eldest daughter, Ibu Rahayu, as spiritually the wisest among us, but she has made it clear that she is only there as a counsellor for those who need her. Cilandak, Bapak's home for many years, is being turned into a cultural and study centre, with the International Archive nearby.

Bapak had laid down that 'neither the spiritual side nor the organisation will fall under the authority of one person, one country or one nation.' Authority and responsibility are vested in a balance of the World Subud Council, the seven zonal representatives and the fourteen international helpers. The location of the executive arm, the International Subud chairman and committee is to rotate as in the past to a new location every four or five years. In January 1989 after the eighth International Congress in Sydney it moved to Tokyo. At the time of writing the international chairman of Subud is Tarzie Varindra Vittachi, until recently deputy director of UNICEF and a Sri Lankan. His deputy, Garrett Thomson, is English and a professor of philosophy.

Two years before he died Bapak had spoken of what would happen when he died:

> You will become responsible. You yourselves will replace Bapak. You yourselves will find the right way to do what is needed. You will be able to sort it out, to guide Subud, but the important thing is always to pray within yourself that Subud will be safe and go on for ever, or at least as long as possible . . . As long as you do what is right, as long as what you do doesn't hurt or disturb anyone else and it is truly good and right, then you will have the protection of Almighty God.[20]

PART TWO

Bapak Speaks

*Chronological selections
from Bapak's talks
given all over the world
between 1958 and 1986.*

B APAK over the years gave thousands of talks to Subud members, some 1700 of which were recorded. He sent messages to congresses and wrote innumerable letters of personal guidance in answer to questions. His insights and guidance touched on all aspects of life – on politics and science, human welfare, commerce and work, culture and the creative arts, sex and marriage and 'secret things'. In all this, Bapak did not give out a new religious teaching or expound a doctrine. Rather, he provided clarifications and explanations of actual or potential experience. Above all, Bapak told of his own experience from a source impossible for us to fathom and which he often said he did not understand himself.

This short selection, given chronologically, is limited broadly to the theme of this book and has been taken out of the middle of often long talks. The present editor would like to be seen as the kind of angler who, when he has hooked a fine fish, draws it into his net. It leaps and twists and glistens for a while, a living thing extracted from nature. Then the angler removes the hook and returns it to the element whence it came and where it has its being. Similarly, these passages (except for the first one) have been lifted out of context and thus deprived of their living continuum, that wide ocean of truth and inner feeling out of which they sprang.

Bapak almost only spoke in the third person. This seems to be because he felt himself to be the impersonal vehicle of what he received, or so that his listeners would not regard him as an 'I'.

Certain Indonesian words, such as *kejiwaan*, *nafsu* and *jiwa*, are sometimes retained (see glossary) because there is no concise English equivalent. The linguistic style of the translations varies, being by different hands.

Only the first piece, the preface to Bapak's main work, *Susila Budhi Dharma*, is complete in itself. *Susila Budhi Dharma* was received by him in the year 1952 in the ancient city of Jogjakarta in Java, as a poem in high Javanese. Bapak himself made a rendering into Indonesian and added this preface.

Bapak's preface to *Susila Budhi Dharma*[1]

To explain the contents of this book it will be best if Bapak first makes clear the conditions under which human beings can receive contact with the Great Life, whose source is in fact the power of God Almighty.

As is evident, God is powerful and far exceeds man in all things; for in very truth He is the Creator of mankind and of heaven and earth. So man as he really is, then, is just a created thing, powerless before God.

Necessarily, since this is his real condition, man cannot with his heart and mind understand or reflect on the nature and power of God. This is why, whenever people try to find a way that may lead to contact with the Great Life, many are stranded on the path or, if not, are impelled – not having a conscious *jiwa* – to stray in other directions, directions which in reality are mirages of the imagination, heart and mind.

So man, in seeking the nature of worship that can make contact with the Great Life, needs above all to stop the welling up of his imagination and thinking. For by doing that he really paralyses his *nafsu* and surrenders his human ability and wisdom; that is to say, the human being obeys and submits with complete sincerity to God Who rules within him.

This in fact is nothing new, for men of old followed this path and found a contact of this quality that they could feel within them. Why, then, are there not many people like that in our own time who still have that contact? The reason is simply that conditions on earth for mankind keep changing as generation succeeds generation, and many people are easily affected by the influence of these ever-changing conditions that face them. Especially has this been so as the human mind has progressively developed its science. This has, as it were, increasingly opened the way for the inner feeling to fall from the realm of inner peace into the realm of thought. In consequence, the human self gradually comes to be ruled more and more by thought, instead of by the quietness of the inner feeling or the inner self, so that in the end man's emotions and brain are always busy and his inner feeling has almost no opportunity to be at peace.

Certainly men must think, for thought is an important tool with which they can strive to fulfil the needs of their life on earth and so make their existence here an orderly one. But to become aware of the *kejiwaan* and make contact again with the Great Life men do not need to use their minds. On the contrary, they should stop the process of their thinking and imagining. For only by so doing can a person receive something from beyond his reach that at length attracts a vibration of energy felt within the self. Clearly, then, the sole way to make contact with the Great Life, or with the power of God, is for a man to surrender sincerely and earnestly. And this surrender must not be in word only, but must penetrate throughout his inner feeling until he truly feels that he believes in, praises and worships no one but God Almighty (Allah).

When he can really do this, at that moment he will also feel powerless, but with no sense of loss, and still conscious.

That is to say, he will feel powerless because at that moment the strength of his *nafsu*, heart and mind will have gone from him; and he will still feel complete because his inner feeling will then be filled with something that comes from the Great Life; finally, he will feel conscious because of the revival of his human *jiwa*.

So it is, if a man can do this in the right way. But when, in his efforts to do this, he keeps using thought because he regards it as a means or tool able to overcome everything, then he can hardly hope that it will be possible to make contact with the Great Life.

This truth was often stated by those who received while living on earth in centuries long past. They said that man's one and only way to be able to draw near to the power of God is that he must be willing to quieten his inner feeling with complete patience, trust and sincerity.

This has been an absolute requirement, for in truth this gift from God can only be received by men who have inner feelings filled with surrender, patience, trust and sincerity before the greatness of God.

The awakening of the human soul[2]

These spiritual exercises of Subud are therefore essentially not a teaching such as can be transmitted from one person to another, but they are an awakening of the soul which has awakened through the power of God and continues to grow by itself. And this awakening of the human soul will eventually bring about integrity, sincerity and health in the being of man. The action of the awakened soul will not only improve the health of the physical body, but the heart, too, will be attuned to what is good and upright; mind and thinking will become capable of faith in the truth, as willed by God for the salvation of man's life, both in this world and in the hereafter.

For it is in the nature of the human soul to bring the internal and external qualities of man into correspondence with its own needs, so that man should be pure both inwardly and outwardly. Once this is achieved, man's external qualities and faculties cease to be barriers to the development of his human soul.

Subud is in accordance with the main religions[3]

However, with the coming of Subud – though Bapak himself does not know its real significance, for it all depends on God's will – God is at work within us, so that we begin to receive and to understand the reality and the practical value of the advice contained in these books: the Zabur, the Torah, the Gospels and the Koran. In Subud, therefore, there is no more need for advice, for theories, for rituals – for the worship of God, for God Himself will guide you as to worship as well as to leading the right kind of life in this world and in the hereafter.

Hence, Subud is not another religion, but it is what God wills for us for the realisation of what is contained in various religions. For those of you who are Christians, once you have received a good deal in Subud, Christianity will become really true for you, because you will see clear proof of its truth, and you will become real Christians. And equally those among you who follow Islam will become true Muslims, and not one of those of whom it is said: 'Muslim yesterday, but not tomorrow' or 'Muslim tomorrow but not the day after'.

Such is the evidence which Bapak has heard from all kinds of people: from Christians, for example, that what they receive and practise in Subud confirms their beliefs, so they say that Subud is entirely in accordance with Christianity. It is the same with the religion of Moses and Abraham: its followers say that Subud fully agrees with what they have read and understood in their books. And thus, too, say the Muslims: that Subud is truly in complete accordance with what is found in the Koran. Thus this Subud latihan is truly man's worship of God, which comes and begins to act by the Will of God at the moment our hearts, desires, and thinking suspend their activity.

Jesus – light to the world[4]

You should not forget that it was only through his surrender and faith in God that Jesus in the end became a light to the world, so that his counsel is of the highest value to mankind. All this was achieved not by learning or through following any theory, but only by following after God.

Be sure, then, that the way in which your senses come into contact with the soul, leading you towards God, is by re-entering the state you experienced as a small child, free from the influences of the external world. It is by the guidance and direction of Almighty God and by liberation from worldly influences that it is possible for you to achieve the condition of the perfected human being. When this is accomplished, then all your inner feelings – mind, heart and all the five senses – will be filled by the Grace of God, acting through the perfected human soul, and so you will be able to use your functions aright, according to the requirements of human life.

And if we were to ascribe human attributes to God we could say that He will then be very pleased and happy, for in this state man can worship Him in all he does, at all times and in all places; and it will be ever clearer and more evident to you how real is the love of God towards man, and also the love of man towards God.

The stillness within movement[5]

Perhaps you would prefer another method; perhaps you wonder why it should be necessary to worship God with this kind of movement, when it is possible to worship God in a quiet, easy way, sitting down, without shouting or moving about, just as other people worship God. But truly – and Bapak wants you to know this – the [spontaneous] movements which you have received and performed do not simply go on like that: these movements serve to free the inner self of its defects, of the dirt which has been brought in through the desires, thoughts and emotions.

Clearly, then, these movements are caused by the process of purification of the inner self from dirt, and the inner self as well as the outer body will thus resume their original condition. And the longer you exercise, the more will this action deepen and broaden, until you will become able to receive in your understanding and finally even in your consciousness.

In this way your inner being will be fitted to follow the movement of life, for life vibrates and moves onwards at great speed, and if you can share in the movement of life it means that you have attained stillness and calm. Let us compare it to flying by plane: though the plane may move at a speed of five hundred miles per hour, yet if you are inside the plane you do not feel its speed, for you share it. It is quite another thing if you are outside a vehicle: it may travel at no more than forty miles per hour, but since you have no share in it you notice its speed as it passes you by.

If, contrary to this, someone wishes that the latihan should be done in stillness, wishes to worship God by stilling everything, although life itself moves so very fast, then, if you wish to worship God while arresting all movement, the highest you can possibly achieve is to watch the whirl of life in its course, without being able to jump on and to move along with the speed of life as it revolves onwards on its path.

Truly, also, although it may be your wish to be still in your worship of God, yet such stillness belongs to the will and effort of emotion, thought and desires. Your body may look still, you may be sitting still, you may not be seeing or hearing what is going on around you, but your thoughts, your emotions, your desires, go on churning inside you. And, thus, all that has been the object of your thinking or emotion presents itself again to your vision. It may be said, therefore, that such stillness is of your outer body only, while your inner being, your thoughts, emotions and desires, are not still at all.

In the Subud latihan, on the other hand, once you are able really to follow the movements you will be able to remain calm while in movement, and you will be calm within calmness. This means that though the wheel of life turns fast you will remain calm on it, and if you stay outside of that wheel you will yet remain calm.

[This passage bears a striking similarity to one in the Gnostic Gospel of Thomas:

51

Jesus said: If they say unto you, 'What is the sign of your Father who is within you?', say to them, 'It is a movement and a rest.' – Ed.]

The meaning of surrender to God[6]

What is it that we have to surrender to God? It is not our wealth, the ones we love, nor whatever else we possess, because God has no need of those things. What we have to surrender is our mind, our heart and our desires, because those are the instruments that form an obstacle to our coming closer to God.

This is what Jesus Christ meant when he said that God will always be with us if we can surrender ourselves to Him and if we can love Him more than anything else, more than ourselves. This means that the love that we have with our hearts and with our feelings is an obstacle that prevents us from coming to the true love of God, because this outer love is only love of things we like to believe we love. But the love that we must have of God must be greater than this.

. . . Only by surrendering himself completely to God, not making use of his mind, his heart or his desires, is there a possibility for man to come into contact with the power of God.

This is what we do in the latihan – we surrender ourselves completely, we do not make use of our mind, heart or desires, but we only accept and receive whatever God sends. So you will understand that Subud is only a symbol of that way of living for man in which he can fulfil the will of God and carry out the will of God for himself in this world and the world to come.

Therefore in the Subud latihan we do not have a teaching; there is nothing we have to learn or do, because all that is required of us is complete surrender. A person who claims to know the way to God is really one who is anticipating God's gifts without having received them.

The only thing we do is surrender ourselves completely and only accept and receive whatever God sends or wants us to have. This is indeed what every prophet has said: 'Surrender yourself entirely, submit completely to God, and then God will take care of you and give you guidance.' In these spiritual exercises we do not expect anything in particular. We do not make for ourselves any image, but we only receive whatever God may send us.

So this divine power, which works in us during the latihan, will bring to each person what is already in himself ... The exercises or latihan of two people can never be the same, because everyone is different from everyone else. Therefore it is clear that there cannot be a theory or a spiritual teaching in Subud because each person is different from another. Whatever he needs and whatever he receives will be different from what somebody else needs and receives. This is why we cannot give any rule or prescription of how to behave when you are in the latihan, because this is something personal for everyone.

Worshipping God in the material world[7]

It may be that there are members who feel, 'Why must the spiritual way be mixed up with money, with enterprises, with undertakings of various kinds. Will that not retard the way of the spirit? Let Bapak explain it like this: the spiritual latihan of Subud is something for mankind and for the heart of man; it is a new kind of spiritual exercise and man's worship of God, and it has appeared at this time when the mind of man is highly developed. From this we can guess and feel that it is the will of God at the present time that while earning our living and attending to worldly matters, and also while close to, or involved in material things, we shall not forget our worship to God because God is with us in all circumstances.

In this, brothers and sisters, Subud is indeed different from other ways. Therefore do not compare it with those others. They are indeed different: in order to have contact with the greatness of God, a man is usually obliged to isolate himself from people, abandon his comforts, and live in some lonely place far away from others, and even if necessary – so they say – to refrain from marrying because he does not need children in order to be able to reach a high spiritual level. This was the usual way in times past. But now it is otherwise. It may be that it is the will of God – and Bapak himself does not understand this – that Subud has appeared at a time when mankind is certainly wholly preoccupied with affairs of this world.

Because of this, we need not at all fear that in handling money we shall come to forget God. No! Brothers and sisters, if you have attained to that which is necessary for your inner being, you can then worship God at the same time as you count money – one, two, three, four . . . While writing a book you will not forget to worship God; while driving a car you will not forget to worship God, and so on, in everything you do. Thus it is clear that the spiritual latihan of Subud is different from other ways, so that we need not worry if we concern ourselves with material things. This means that Subud is not isolated from anything.

Jesus feeds the thousands; the need for social work[8]

Do not be mistaken and think that when someone gives gladly he will come to poverty and misery. Not at all! Someone who truly gives with sincerity will receive many times what he has given. Jesus is again the example. When Jesus went up into the mountain, thousands of people followed him and, because those thousands were very hungry and had nothing to eat, they asked him, 'Jesus, if you are really the child of God, beloved by God, you will surely be able to give us food, for we are hungry.' Well, how could Jesus give food to thousands of people who followed him when he himself had none and had brought none with him? Then, without knowing how it happened, Jesus was given a piece of bread, just one piece of bread, hardly enough for one person. But, through the grace of God, it could be broken again and again and given to the thousands who followed him, and what they received satisfied them – truly a miracle!

This is a symbol and an example for us, because what was done by Jesus is indeed symbolic. Jesus was willing to give to mankind, to others, and so when he gave to one person he received enough for one; when he gave to a thousand he received for a thousand; and when he gave to ten thousand he received also enough for ten thousand. That is why Bapak said just now, do not be mistaken and think that if you are willing to give, you will then become poor – no! If you really give with all your heart and with real sincerity, you will be able to receive more than you have given. This is indeed what Bapak himself has experienced in his life and in the lives of other people.

. . . Bapak always says to you that the way of the Subud spiritual latihan is not different from the way of the religions. For religion and the Subud spiritual latihan are a struggle of man to worship Almighty God and to serve his fellow men on earth. So it is right and proper for us to carry out social work; in other words, to be active in the social field. Care for the sick, help for the hungry and for those who are undernourished and deprived – help, that is, for the poor people – and help for neglected children: all this is social work. It is excellent for us to undertake such things because it is very right that, besides worshipping God, we work for human society on earth.

Therefore, brothers and sisters, on the organisational side in Subud we need gradually to create a body which can fulfil the social tasks which we will undertake – in the care of the sick, of the hungry, or neglected children. This is our fundamental aim, in addition to our worship of God.

Bapak says that social work is very compatible with what we receive in the latihan and what we do in our worship towards God, because social work provides ways or activities in which our hearts and emotions will be educated to love and help our fellow men. Social work is a sign of the compassion of men towards other men, of the close connection between men in their feelings towards one another; it is the sign of the link between one soul and another.

Therefore, do not worry if you give something away. Of course, Bapak does not want to urge you to spend your money – not at all! But your very needs in your worship towards God require you to combine the two ways – the outer with the inner, the inner with the outer – that is, worship of God with work in the social field.

If we are truly submitted to God so that we become empty, all our 'property' disappears; and that which constitutes this 'property' within us is nothing more nothing less, and nothing other than our thinking and our heart. Our thinking and our hearts are our property – our worldly wealth. If we leave heart and thoughts behind us we become a very poor person in this world. We renounce them so that we can receive from God. How can God put something into you if, within, you are still full of material possessions? If you are still full of desire and thought, the gift from God cannot enter. It is different if your house is empty. If your house is already empty, God gives to you and this receiving from God will make ready that which is in your house – in other words, in yourself. Then you will know and understand the difference between the content – the content of thinking and desires – and the content of the gift of God. So we are not surprised at the words of Jesus Christ: 'All that is on earth and all that is beyond the earth is within me.' That means that whatever riches there are exist within him. How could this be? It is because the bodily nature of Jesus Christ was empty and so filled with the power of God that he could know everything which cannot ordinarily be known.

In your own interest, for the progress of your own soul and inner feeling, you need to improve yourselves, and the method of correction is none other than worship of God and work for the social needs of our human society.

Follow the examples of Muhammad and Jesus; Jesus' suffering⁹

[*Shortened version. The first three paragraphs were not recorded, but remembered and written down afterwards*].

Before you are able to help others, you helpers should yourselves show an attitude of patience, fortitude and surrender in facing difficulties. These difficulties which you meet and which are sometimes felt as illness, are caused by the purification process which is taking place in your inner feeling. There is really already evidence that well-being and happiness will come about if man is willing to follow this path which will confront him with many difficulties and sufferings. The way back to God, which is the way to pureness and holiness, cannot be without suffering and sacrifices.

Don't think that Bapak had not to suffer. Bapak too had to undergo suffering and sacrifices, and went through a time when he could not even take care of his family, nor even of himself.

. . . For you Christians the life of Jesus should be an example, for Jesus too had to suffer from the moment he was born until the moment he was crucified. But he faced difficulties and illness – for he too fell ill – with patience and he even thanked God, because he knew why and for what he had to suffer. But you, as soon as you feel ill, you are worried, you quickly run to the doctor and are afraid. Just this feeling of fear and worry will easily make you more ill.

. . . And for you who are Christians, the life of Jesus Christ should really be more than just an example. You should really become able to follow as much as possible in his footsteps. In the same way, for Muslims – for example Bapak – the prophet Muhammad is the perfect example whom it is necessary to follow.

Therefore you should be able to carry out what the messengers of God in former times have preached, and the advice they have given. But you should not follow the teaching of Jesus (or of any religion) with words only, and with your minds, but rather with deeds and with the whole of your lives. The commandments and directions of Almighty God should not remain just words for you.

. . . You have all been given God's grace. Truly that is a very privileged situation, for with God's help you will become able to put into practice what we are taught in religion.

Although the latihan is guided by Almighty God, and is His work in us, it is still very necessary that we try hard to be peaceable and loving in our daily lives. We should try to be especially peaceable and loving so that we can meet any difficulties or unpleasantnesses that may come our way, with serenity. In Islam, such a way of being is called *amal*.

For this reason, you must be prepared for many sacrifices, and it will take a long time for you to come so far as to be able truly to face the difficulties in your lives with patience and inner peace.

And since you are not yet really able to live out this *amal*, your reward from God will be proportionate. If your willingness and ability to follow the will of God is only forty percent, then, when you die, that will be the proportion of the heavenly reward which God will be able to give you.

With Jesus Christ, it was quite different. He was really one hundred percent purified, and when he died and went to heaven he was able to enter his Father's Kingdom, to return to his Father completely, one hundred percent.

Everything you have heard about the life of Jesus, from his birth and childhood onwards, until his crucifixion, is truly a sign, representing what he had to suffer. And we too should be prepared to accept sacrifice and suffering in our lives, just as Jesus took them upon himself here on earth.

We cannot imagine what it can mean, how it can feel, to be crucified. If you think about the difficulties in your own lives – perhaps you do not have a good job, or your work is not going well, or you have no money, or you are sick – how can there be any comparison with the sufferings of Jesus Christ? You should not think that Jesus was never sick. When he was, as did happen, he would say, 'Abba, Father', with love and gratitude.

Through the latihan you will become able to fathom the mysteries of this life, which you cannot understand as yet. For all the mysteries of life are in God's hand; but when you reach the state of a perfected human being, they will all unveil themselves for you.

When you have reached this state, the sign of the cross will be in you, a cross that can never be taken from you, that will always be with you, and in you, and will still be part of you when you die and enter the next world. Amen.

The latihan is the worship of one God of mankind[10]

Further, what happens in the latihan is truly a receiving, and it can be received by each one, but differently between one and another, yet in accordance with the inner self of each one. For instance, people of the religion of Islam, as with the population of Indonesia, receive Subud in accordance with whatever is within them, and what is in their inner self, so that their religion and their national characteristic is not diminished. It can be received in the way which is their customary way of life. It is the same with people from other nations, for instance America. Their latihan is received in the way which is in accordance with their inner self, so that they do not imitate Indonesians, or the way of Islam, or any other national characteristics.

And so in Subud there can be and there is made possible a uniting of religions, of streams, because after receiving this spiritual latihan, people feel that man has truly only one aim, that is worship to the One God of mankind. Thus it is not worship to Gods of different kinds, no! It is worship of One God for mankind! The nature of the spiritual latihan of Subud is a technique, that is, a technique of everything that has been said and heard, and thought and followed (in the different religions), and with the birth of Subud you and the brothers of the different religions are able to know the truth of what has been said and followed in the religions and streams of each one.

What has happened in Subud is really not something new – that means it is only new now at the time of receiving. But it is something that has existed when man came to this earth. How can man forget what he had, what truly was brought down when God created this world? Because as the days, the months and the years go on, with the change of the epochs, man's thinking quickly progresses, so that with the quickening of the thinking, man forgets his *jiwa*, forgets God, and forgets that life is created by God, and that everything he has within him is all under the protection and will of the power of God.

[In connection with the development of culture Bapak also said. 'What God loves is your own nature and not what you imitate, so if you develop your national characteristics you will be close to God and the result will be no hatred of one nation for one another.' Ed.]

On Buddhists and Hindus in Subud[12]

. . . Such, in brief, is the *latihan kejiwaan* of Subud. And so, with regard to a Subud brother of the Buddhist or Hindu religion, if his inner feeling is no longer influenced by the *nafsu* and if his thinking mind is no longer tempted to think of all kinds of things, then, inasmuch as the Buddhist or Hindu religion has become what he believes in and has also become included in the capacity and state of his inner self, he will certainly get clarifications in his receiving about the real meaning of what is obtained in his religion.

In your letter you mention that in the latihan you always say the name of the Dewas and several times you pronounced mantras which you had learned. Indeed, such things are not wrong, because all of that has become your faith, your capacity and the condition of your inner as a person of the Buddhist or Hindu religion. In fact, the condition which you mention is the actual result of what you have learned and believe. Gradually, the condition you mention will become clearer and clearer and more apparent until you will be opened in your inner self and be aware and able to see that your life is truly to face the power of God which envelops the whole universe.

Therefore religion, in its outer aspect, is in fact a guidance so that man may be able, with that guidance, to act nobly or be imbued with a noble character; and afterwards, if possible, the awareness and consciousness of his inner self will face the power of God, which envelops the entire universe. In religion, what is set forth above is called the *hakekat* [the truth or reality].

That is Bapak's clarification. As yet, Bapak cannot give further explanations because the time has not yet arrived for you. Therefore Bapak hopes that you will just be patient, because patience is the important condition which protects you from confusion and which will make possible the smooth process of purification of the inner-self and the development of your *jiwa*.

[*Extract from a letter*]

On fasting by Jesus and Muhammad[13]

In reality, Lent and Ramadhan have equal value. Christians feel that fasting in Lent is very important for them because it is derived and adapted from what was done and experienced by Jesus Christ.

You say that Jesus Christ carried out the religious observance of fasting in the wilderness for forty days at the time of Lent. This may be taken to mean that Jesus Christ fasted during this time so that his inner feeling might be swept clean of the influence of the forces causing darkness – wilderness – within.

For Muslims, the religious observance of fasting in the month of Ramadhan is the same. This too is derived and adapted from what was done and experienced by the prophet Muhammad. It is told that the prophet Muhammad fasted in a cave at that time – this too means in darkness. He carried out the religious observance of fasting in the cave so that the inner feeling could be swept clean of the influence of *nafsu* causing darkness. It is therefore said that the revelation that he was to be the messenger of God came to him in the cave. In other words, it was then that he received the first command of the One God.

This is Bapak's explanation concerning these two religious observances of fasting, as seen from the spiritual point of view. So Bapak feels that Lent and Ramadhan are of equally great and high value.

Furthermore, any individual Christians, or Christians in general, may follow the religious observance of fasting during Ramadhan if they wish to do so, because, although this is not usually customary for Christians, if the fast is observed it is also a method whereby the influence of the *nafsu*, which always constitutes a temptation and a hindrance to the quiet of the inner feeling, can be separated and swept away from the inner feeling. Conversely, it is the same for Muslims who wish to carry out the religious observance of fasting during Lent.

Now, of course, you ask: how is it for us or for Subud members? Bapak would like you to know that, because our brotherhood of Susila Budhi Dharma consists of members of various nationalities and religions, it is best for each member to observe the fast of his own religion unless he wishes to observe another as well.

[Extract from a letter]

Fasting and the need for forgiveness[14]

Usually after fasting for twenty days you are able to feel the result of your fast. It will not cause you to get some money or have a bigger income or a higher rate of pay or to obtain an annual bonus – no! When people receive the *qodar* that is sent down, their hearts and their feelings become good. For instance, out of the inner feeling will grow a feeling of affection, of love, of being close to other people and also a feeling of loving-kindness towards one's fellow men, so that eventually this feeling will be expressed in a readiness to give *zakat fitroh*, or alms, which means giving something to other people who are in need.

That is why people in general, and all of you, very much need to fast. It is necessary for you to train yourselves to become people filled with love and loving-kindness for your fellow men and liking to help people who need help. In [the Islamic] religion this quality is called the fourth pillar, or foundation – that is, *zakat* and *fitroh*.

Besides that, the character of the *qodar* that has been received in the inner feeling also causes you to feel that you yourself have often wronged your fellow men, especially your parents and the older members of your family. And that is why in due course all of you need to go to one another to ask for forgiveness for all your wrong deeds and to have your friends and relatives do likewise to you. You also need to ask for blessing and forgiveness from your parents, asking them to forgive you so far as possible for what you may have done to them. For people will not be able to avoid doing wrong; they are bound to do something wrong, though not all the time.

From the relief and satisfaction to their hearts, the other people will then feel an affection for you which was lacking before you asked their forgiveness; this is truly being helpful. By the grace and mercy of God, this also broadens and widens your path in life, so that, for instance, it becomes generally easier to make efforts and accomplish what you set out to do. For it is as if there were no thorny barriers in your way. And, that being so, it also means that almost everyone, as it were, blesses your life, blesses your way of life as long as you live in this world.

Apart from the fact that you will eventually come to feel loving-kindness and affection towards your fellow men, you will also know and be able to grasp how the *nafsu* go round and about in your inner feeling. In this way you will afterwards cease to be one hundred percent controlled by these *nafsu* or used as their tools or be tossed around by them. What is more, you will be able to manage them.

And hence you will eventually be able to do things of a worldly nature, such as earning your living, running a business, keeping a shop, and so on, yet your heart and feelings will be full of love towards your fellow men. Nor will you seek a huge profit when that profit would be harmful to other people.

Experiences of a maharishi in Subud[15]

People are always asking what religion Subud is. But Bapak answers and replies that Subud is not a religion. It is the Subud members who have religions. When Subud members who belong to the religion of Islam enter Subud, they receive the latihan in accordance with what is taught in Islam. When Subud members who are Catholics enter Subud, in receiving the *latihan kejiwaan* they are guided and led by God towards the perfection of the Catholic faith. It is the same for Subud members who are Protestants, and also for members of other religions, such as Buddhists, Hindus and so on.

Bapak has often told you about the member from India who had spent thirty-seven years in the study of religious matters; in fact he had become a maharishi after thirty years of practising *samadhi* [meditation]. But about three weeks after he had entered Subud, quite by chance Bapak was in New Delhi for a while, and one night after latihan, when this member was in a state of quietness and emptiness, he saw the Buddha shining before him. He immediately fell on his knees and worshipped.

Then he said to Bapak, 'I thank Bapak very much indeed for his guidance and for leading me to be able to find what I always dreamed of seeing – that is, to see the Buddha in shining light.' Bapak answered, 'It was not Bapak who guided you, but God Himself Who guides you in your *jiwa*, so that you can know how Buddha truly is who is full of light.' And it is also the same for Subud members of the Christian and Islamic religions, including Bapak himself.'

The proof of God's love for man[16]

You have to prove to yourself that God loves man.

Every year after the end of the Ramadhan fast, people are shouting, '*Allahu akbar! Allahu akbar!*' – 'God is Great! God is Great!'; '*Laillaha illala, laillaha illala wa ilham*' – 'There is no God but God and the grace of God.'

And Bapak asks, What is the use of shouting it? Prove it! Once you have done with shouting about it, do something to prove it to us. Is it true that God loves man? Or is it just something we say? Where is the proof of God's love for man? The proof lies in releasing all the wealth God has given to man [for that purpose], and in arranging a life for man that is not full of complaints and shortages and suffering but is truly prosperous, just and peaceful in this world. That is the proof of God's love.

Until you have been able to achieve that, there is no use in saying God loves man, because you have no evidence.

Culture that comes from emptiness[17]

People in general still treat religion as something ordinary or something which is just an everyday practice. But those who can receive, those who are able to find that inner reality of the Koran or the Bible, are then able to obtain a proof, an outer proof, in the form of what can be seen as culture. In the Christian church, for example, people have received music to accompany Christian worship. This is something that was originally received in the way that we receive the *latihan kejiwaan*.

Similarly, in Islam and in all religions there is a culture that accompanies the religion. This culture originates from the inner self or the life that is free from the influence of the passions. Bapak knows that this culture or movement of the inner self when it is free from the influence of the *nafsu* is something that was much easier to receive in the olden days than it is now. Today we have the cinema, radio and television; we have the newspapers; we have all sorts of things going on around us all the time.

This means that our ability to receive from within is very limited. In the olden days there wasn't any of this, only ordinary life. People were much more sensitive and it was easier for them to receive what is called the sound of silence, or the sound of death. The meaning of the 'sound of death' is that it is a sound or movement or life that comes from nothing, or emptiness. In the olden days people were much more sensitive to this and much more able to receive it. But today, since we have received the latihan, that is what we receive through the latihan. We are able to sing, to move, to dance, all from something that is free from the influence of the passions and the influence of the heart and mind.

When in time this movement which we receive goes deeper into ourselves and beyond the realm of the feeling – that is, the thing that beats up there [Bapak points to the physical heart] – it goes deeper, to the 'heart' that is actually located in the liver and we will begin to experience that there is a balance in that feeling. When the latihan has spread to that level, when we are happy we will also experience, parallel to our happiness, a feeling of sadness. When we are very depressed we will experience a parallel feeling of joy.

When we reach that point our feelings will always be balanced. We will never experience joy without sadness or sadness without joy in other words, we will never overbalance; we will always be in balance. This is something of enormous value for our lives, because actually all danger comes from man's sadness or happiness. Most mistakes are made by people when they are very, very happy.

Man cannot understand God; on Sufism[18]

The *latihan kejiwaan* is something that cannot be thought about, cannot be analysed and cannot be understood with the mind. It exists and comes from beyond the mind; and that is the reason why Bapak continues still to travel, still to come and talk to you all over and over again, to remind you that the latihan is something from beyond the mind, and cannot be subjected to the analysis of the mind or to the prompting and direction of the mind.

For example, in Islam there are teachings about the meaning of life, about the meaning of Heaven and Hell and God, called the Sufi tradition. There are many kinds of Sufi, among them for example the Naqshbandi, which Bapak was acquainted with when he was young. They teach you in the form of a theory. Everything is analysed. They tell you, This is the being of man; within man's being there is this kind of spirit; this kind of *roh* is here; this kind of life force is here; this is here; this is the Power of God; and you can go from here to here in this way and that way; and if you do this and that, so and so will happen.

And when you listen to it, when you hear these teachings, you get the feeling it must be true, it is so clear and well-expressed. And yet the fact is that it is not true, and it cannot be true. Because it would imply that man with his heart and mind can analyse and understand the power of Almighty God. And that is clearly not possible. If man can do that, it is not the power of God but a figment of man's imagination.

All of this teaching, like that of the Naqshbandi, these matters that are explained in such detail – man cannot know these things, man cannot explain them. If they can be explained, then it is only God who can explain them to man. But the point is, when God explains them He does not do it in that way, in the way explained by the Sufi teachers . . . Do not mistake these teachings for the reality; the reality is what is contained in the latihan.

God's will is that human beings feel as one[19]

At one time the most experienced helper residing in Singapore was Edward van Hien, who happened to be a Christian. It was his duty at that time to go and open applicants in Malaysia who had heard about Subud and had asked to be opened. And Edward travelled there with two or three assistants, one of whom was a Hindu and the other a Muslim, and in the normal way opened the people who had asked for the contact. Bapak thinks maybe there were about twelve of them and, not surprisingly, being in Malaysia, they were all Muslims. Edward van Hien opened them, reminding them that God was Almighty and that there was no power to be worshipped except Almighty God, to whom they should simply surrender themselves fully.

They were all able to receive the latihan. In their latihan some of them began to recite the Koran and to receive many things which seemed to them to confirm the reality of Subud since it was in line with their faith in Islam. They were impressed and very much affected by this. Afterwards they came to Edward and said, 'What you have given us is something of great value. Are you also a Muslim like us, that you are able to bring this to us? He said, 'No, not at all. I am a Christian.'

. . . Having received Subud, we can work out what may be the purpose behind it: which is that, in today's world, it is no longer appropriate for there to be a separation between people of different religions, different nationalities, different races. We have the proof in Subud in the *latihan kejiwaan* that it is not God's will that men should be separate, that men should put a distance between each other in their feelings, a distance resulting because they belong to different religions. Or, even more than that, a distance resulting from which social stratum they belong to. God wills that human beings should feel as one, as one human race, all with the same direction.

That was what was experienced by these people in Malaysia who were opened by a Christian and then received the content of Islam. What they found was that we are all human beings with a common direction and aim: towards the One Almighty God.

The latihan is not the copyright of Subud[20]

This is the purpose and this is the process of the *latihan kejiwaan* of Subud. Actually we should not really say 'of Subud'. That makes it sound as if it is only in Subud that you can receive God's grace, or the guidance of God; or that it is only in Subud that you can receive the revelations of God, which is not the case.

The fact is that anyone who truly surrenders to God with patience, acceptance and sincerity can receive the *latihan kejiwaan*. It is not the 'copyright' of Subud. It is very important to be aware of this, for no one can lay claim to God. If we can understand that, it will make us tolerant. It will make us accepting of other people, we won't consider ourselves special; and that is actually the aim of the *latihan kejiwaan*.

Why members must also practise their religion[21]

Now the most important thing for all of us is the latihan . . . It is a receiving that should fill our whole being. It is to exercise our *jiwa*, to bring our *jiwa* to life. Apart from that we need an exercise for our physical selves, and that is why we have religion and religious observances. For that reason Bapak wants to warn you not to have the misconception that when we are opened in Subud we don't need to practise our religion any more, that is all right to forget about our five daily prayers or, if you are a Christian, the observance of the Christian religion. To do that would mean that you separate yourself from your fellows.

. . . It is very important for you to be aware of this, especially the helpers; to understand and not mislead people by saying that 'the latihan is enough, you don't have to practise your religion'. If this happens it will lead to a decline in your *jiwa*, a decline in the spiritual.

. . . So, brothers and sisters, it is a fact of enormous good fortune for you – one without comparison – that you have been able to receive the *latihan kejiwaan*. Because the one who works in the *latihan kejiwaan* is the power of Almighty God. If it was not this power that acts, it would be completely impossible for you to be cleansed of the sins and the traces of wrong doing and the dirt that is within your being.

Bapak says 'within your being', which is not just the body but also your imagination, your feelings and your fine nervous feeling. All that is being cleansed little by little through the working of God's power. So it is very important for you to do the *latihan kejiwaan*, and to do it with a feeling of patience, submission and acceptance.

And besides doing your latihan in the way Bapak has described, you must not neglect the practice of your religion and whatever your religion prescribes. This way your outer also benefits; your physical body, your outer everyday activities, and your work and your relationships with other people will also benefit.

Bapak's prayer[22]

Almighty God, we kneel before thee in worship.
Please grant us the grace of a pure heart.
Please protect us from temptation and bring us close to heaven.
Please grant us the wisdom of a human being in this world,
And we ask that in the next we may one day stand before Thee.
Amen.

Ibu Rahayu speaks about religion[23]

During a visit to Britain in 1990, Bapak's daughter Ibu Rahayu (see page 9) said the following in answer to members' questions about their problems with religion.

There is no religion that is not right, because at the core each religion is true, and as we go through the latihan process it can happen to us that we have experiences about one religion or another and these can come to us without us seeking them – they just happen; we come to an understanding perhaps of the Christian religion. We may then have an understanding about the Muslim religion. So there isn't a guideline in Subud about which religion you should belong to, because that depends upon your own beliefs.

You can liken a religion to wearing a shirt – a shirt for the soul. There is one shirt that is the Christian shirt which the soul can put on, and there's another shirt which is the Muslim shirt; and if you have an experience of being attracted by one religion and then attracted by another and you stay a Muslim or go back to Christianity, it doesn't actually matter. The important thing is, you should follow the religion that you believe.

You should never feel that one particular group or individual has a better connection or has a better latihan, because for each of us it is the same, it is between us and Almighty God.

So don't get the idea, for example, that by being a Muslim you will be closer to God, or by being a Christian you will be closer to God. Because all depends on your condition and the power of Almighty God.

So when we follow our religion we should follow the religion that we believe in, and through the *latihan kejiwaan* we will be able to get from that religion that which we really hope for.

So if for example you don't have a religion, you shouldn't feel that it's not necessary to have a religion – and similarly if you have a religion, you shouldn't have any concern or fear about the nature of the latihan.

When asked about Christ being the only *Son of God, Ibu Rahayu answered quite simply:*

There is a meaning that Christ is the only Son of God, which you will be able to find through doing the latihan and being a Christian.

PART THREE

Experiences and evidences

For reasons of space, only a third of the contributions sent in have been included. The choice was often difficult, for the content in one often overlapped with the content in another. My apologies to those disappointed.

All writers were asked to address themselves only to the theme of Subud and religion. The result, sometimes shortened, is thus only a segment of the total likely experiences of each as Subud members. Individual styles have been preserved.

Several contributors have subsequently told me that they have 'moved on' since they wrote their piece into a new stage of understanding and would write it somewhat differently now. This is not surprising for, as a theologian puts it in the final evidence, religion is here seen more as process than possession.

Subud and Catholic Life as one

The very first aspect of my life in which I felt changes after I started doing the latihan was precisely in my observance of my religion. I had known about Subud members in the Catholic Church, like Père Bescond. The Subud spiritual counsellor of Brazil was a practising Catholic who had spoken to her confessor before joining Subud and had been given permission to do so. I felt no need to speak to any priest now about my joining Subud.

The first result was that gradually it became easier for me to go to Confession and Holy Communion more frequently. It was really important for me to do so. My mind which beforehand used to torture me with petty little details slowly became calmer and steadier. A few times (it was never when I wanted it to happen) I felt such lovely perfume coming from the Eucharist while I was in the queue to receive Holy Communion.

I began to experience the joy and happiness of being a Catholic in Subud and how Mass and Holy Communion helped my latihan and vice-versa. I found similarities between what occurred to me during my daily prayer of the rosary and the latihan. As in the first minutes of the latihan, during the first three mysteries of the rosary I seemed to be throwing a lot of rubbish out, and the last two mysteries were very calm and peaceful as usually occurs in the last minutes of the latihan.

Gradually my Subud life and my Catholic life became truly one. On one occasion, as I was doing the latihan (it was July 15th), suddenly I found myself saying, 'Tomorrow – Our Lady of Carmel.' I had been completely unaware of the date and had forgotten all about the Feast of Our Lady of Carmel on the following day, but the latihan reminded me of it. Many times at church, especially in the Chapel of the Holy Eucharist, I have felt the strong vibration of the latihan.

To my surprise, in the latihan I began to recite long stretches of prayers in Latin which I had completely forgotten. I used to repeat those prayers by rote at the convent school when I was a little girl and hardly knew what they meant. Now, in the latihan, I was aware of their content, and it was so pleasant to be saying them! My first latihan after I had been approved as a helper was a joyful chanting of the Magnificat, a prayer I had hardly been aware of before, and which suddenly I found to be deeply engraved within me. Also, gradually prayers of the Mass and passages of the Holy Testament started opening a treasure of meanings to me. Each time I read them I discovered something new I had not seen there before.

Another lovely experience has been to hear my Jewish sisters saying Christian prayers during latihan, and the Christian sisters saying Jewish ones, both saying Islamic ones, and so on. How gratifying it is to have Jewish, Protestant, Catholic and non-sectarian people of all ages worshipping God together like real brothers and sisters.

LB
This was originally composed as a letter for members in Poland

A German Protestant is enfolded in grace

I have realised that I was 'a Christian' ever since I was a small child. However, at that time it was only with God the Father that I felt a living relationship – the Creator of the world and all of glorious nature, the contemplation of which always made my feelings wide, and lifted me into a state of worship. I believed in and experienced Him as the God of Love, the only one who is really able to love, especially when I suffered under my own inability, and that of those closest to me, to be truly loving. Jesus Christ was only an idea for me at that time, and I was not able to pray to him.

When, at the age of forty I became a Subud applicant, I said to the woman helper, 'One condition – if I come to Subud, I must still be able to keep my Christian religion.' She looked tranquilly at me, and said, 'You will find your way into it far more deeply.'

A little while after my opening, I found that I was no longer able to pray in words. At first this worried me, but an inner voice said. 'Trust, and let go.' In the 'letting go' I felt deeply relaxed, looked forward to every latihan, and felt a powerful current of strength and help. Later, prayer returned in another form, and the words were accompanied with melodies from the latihan, and circling movements throughout my body, especially in my feet.

After about fifteen years, I began to say 'Musa' and 'Isa' [Moses and Jesus – Ed.] very often in my latihan. Sometimes, when I said

'Isa' there would be a sudden bright light in my head. Later on, when I said 'Isa' the light would appear in the region of my heart.

During this period I went through a very troubled time. I had had many testing times through the years, and had always reminded myself of Bapak's twelve years of difficulties and trials. I would often repeat the words he had once sung:

> Do not always listen to your heart, but become free of its promptings, both good and bad. Let your heart sit quietly at the feet of the soul and at the feet of Almighty God.

I had long been able to feel the difference between the feelings of my heart and those of my inner-feeling, but however well I knew, however aware I was, the heart-feelings were so strong! My sorrow was such that I thought, 'My heart will break,' and sometimes it flowed over into fury and despair.

Then, suddenly, came something incredible, something completely new. At night, as I lay down to sleep, and tried to be quiet, there He was – Jesus. He was around me, and in me, and all my trouble was washed away and I felt nothing but peace and protection.

Most nights, there then arose – and still does today – a prayer in me, a song with a very simple melody: 'You are with me, I am with You,' with these circling movements in my body, soft and gentle movements like rocking a baby.

It was the reality of the 'prayer of the heart' – 'Lord Jesus Christ, Son of the living God, enfold me in your Grace' – it was this being enfolded that I felt.

Later there were other words of prayer, always with very simple melodies: 'Praise and honour, praise and thanks,' or, over and again, 'God the Father, God the Son and God the Holy Ghost.'

I have experienced that God sends us difficulties, but that in them, and specifically through them, He can give us wonderful help.

My trouble has passed, but when I am quiet I still feel this Presence. What the helper said at the very beginning has come true. What was words before in St Matthew: – 'I am with you always, even unto the end of the world' – has become reality.

VR

Holy Bread, consolation and Hebrew song

In my experience of the practice of my religion, Roman Catholicism, and the spiritual latihan of Subud I can only say that the two go together as if they had been brothers always. The latihan has really given me a much deeper appreciation of the working of the Sacraments. For example, every time I take the Holy Bread I experience a widening feeling within and an inner peace. Sometimes words of consolation speak through me after Communion.

Another thing: although I have no Jewish ancestors, I find myself singing Hebrew in my latihan. Who knows, perhaps my soul feels Jewish? I am very happy and very much my natural self when I sing 'Adonai' with the expressive emotion of Jewishness. I have also been led to be open to the Jewish Law and to make a synthesis with the Gospels.

EG

Everything in spite of me

I am an ordained Anglican priest and a member of Subud and have long since given up any attempt to maintain an 'intellectual' approach to religion. I am not sure that I have ever had such an approach and I am very troubled by other people's desire to argue about words. What we believe is insignificant in comparison with what we believe in. And I feel that worship finally finds shape in silence. I am too old for the youngsters who want to spend their time together strumming guitars and singing what I would call jingles. Religion and God are not the same thing. I am even troubled by Bapak's apparently endless explanations. For someone who has no teaching to give he does have a great deal to say. No doubt, though, he has a great deal more right to say anything than I do.

As a priest, I am set in a particular place, a hospital where some ministry is expected of me. Again, my personal feeling is that this is ludicrous. If anything is accomplished it must surely be by act of God. There are those who express their pleasure, gratitude and satisfaction with my presence, and those who do the reverse. I am able to be with people at the human level in their pain and grief, even in their relief and wonder. But I do not see anything positive arising from, say, faithfulness, courage or perseverance in me. Everything is in spite of me. I fail constantly, and yet I feel I must just get on with life and 'leave it all to God', hoping He won't finally write me off.

I want simplicity, but how I love my comforts! I have to live a public life, but I want to hide! There is endless work, but I am lazy! I wear the outward show of a Christian in a way that arouses all sorts of expectations; inwardly I can only be me and, thank God, sometimes I manage to let that show through.

Experiences, too, can be deceptive. Aren't we told how deceitful the human heart is? So also are the human eyes, the human mind. The angel of light may only be wearing fancy dress. Am I a cynic? Certainly absurd!

For what, then, can I be more grateful than the opportunity to allow Almighty God to take over, to inform and re-interpret what I imagined was already His? If the words 'living religion' mean anything it can only be that man is truly in submission to the living God.

CC

On observing Lent

I am writing this because of my growing Christian faith and because of the articles published on this subject in *Subud News*. It seems that I am not alone in my experiences of turning to my own background rather than to a new culture and understanding.

Three years ago I fasted in Ramadhan for the last time, and throughout the fast at regular intervals a voice would ask me quietly and clearly, 'Why are you not fasting in Lent? We are waiting for you.'

Last year in Oslo I began to observe Lent together with my father and one other friend. This year there were four of us. We follow it as we receive it is right; prior to Lent this year and last year we tested together how it should be observed. Since that last Ramadhan I have had many Christian experiences, especially concerning Mary. I know that Subud is changing now and developing into something really honest within each of the world's cultures, something that really belongs to each place in which it is practised, at the same time as it is omnipresent in its strength and values. If it ever was abstract (especially to the outside world), it is no longer so. I feel enormous pleasure in the knowledge that it is now something much more matter-of-fact.

We have gone about the practice of Lent quite simply: six hours of sleep, half an hour reading the Bible with fifteen minutes of prayer before and after – each morning. Simple food, with no sweet foods or jams. Nothing between meals. No sweets, cigarettes, alcohol or anything like that, and regular weekly church-going. No meat of any kind – or fish. I look forward to the celebration of Easter all the more.

FL

An incredible Christmas present

Late one Christmas Eve I had a strong feeling to go to church for the midnight service. I had not been to church for over ten years.

As a child I had been taken regularly and as an adolescent I had yearned to get closer to some inner understanding I felt was just outside my grasp. At last when I was fifteen I had been prepared for confirmation; I had prayed so hard and earnestly! Finally, the day came; in my white dress I went forward to be blessed by the bishop, full of expectancy, my head vivid with the New Testament account of the pentecostal flame. The bishop's hand, emerging from lace ruffles, was laid on my head. I waited. I went back to my pew. The service ended. Nothing was changed. I knew no more, I felt no more. So time went on – I attended Holy Communion every other Sunday, early. I felt it was my fault I experienced no change, but that I must persevere.

So I did, for two years. For all the outer ritual, no matter how I prayed or tried, there was nothing there for me.

I searched in other places, other religions: Quakers, Zen, Yoga, Gurdjieff and others; a brief taste and I always knew, 'This is not my path – it is not changing me inside at all.'

Then, in my mid-twenties, in Chelsea public library, I found *The Path of Subud* by Husein Rofé. As I read it I knew that everything I felt could be possible, was. I found the central London group and joined as simply as a fish being tipped back into a river after being trapped in a jam-jar.

So after about four years of experiencing the grace of the latihan, I felt to go to church. I followed my feelings.

Chelsea Old Church is a small and simple church, beside the Thames, upstream from the centre of London. It was built at least 900 years ago. It had been quite badly damaged in the war but restored with love. Walking along the embankment in the cool Christmas Eve night, I saw it lit up, golden light pouring from its windows. As I went inside I was amazed to find it was packed solid, I had to find a seat in the gallery. The white walls shone and the candelabra bathed everything with gold. The atmosphere was so alive and happy with family groups of all ages and a feeling of expectancy in the air.

The service started, the traditional Christmas carols and readings and prayers. There was no trace of the mournful, grey atmosphere of the dim, gothic churches sparsely attended by a faded few I had remembered from years back. It was so light and happy.

Eventually the service reached a point where communion was offered to those that wished. I looked down from the gallery to the busy line of worshippers who waited to receive the sacrament. I was surprised, I had not expected communion to be at this service. It was so long since I had chosen to stop going to church that I thought I had no right to join the queue. But then I went down. No one knew me. Everyone seemed so happy and accepting; God would understand, I reasoned, it was a sentimental journey.

Finally, I was kneeling at the altar rail, quietly waiting as the clergymen moved slowly along. The first with the waifer of bread, the second with the chalice of wine. The old ritual, I knew how it was. The clergyman was there, placing the bread on my tongue.

The most ecstatic joy poured through my body with the intensity of an electric shock. My mind had barely started to comprehend this incredible sensation than the chalice was touching my lips and I sipped the wine. Thorough anguish beyond all pain imaginable suffused me. Then it was gone.

I stood up and returned to my place in a daze. The service continued. I marvelled at the totally unexpected experience and thanked God for such an incredible Christmas present.

MS

Gentleness of the Sacrament

I am sure I am one of many for whom understanding of the Christian faith has been illuminated by the latihan. I grew up rejecting confirmation as I did not then feel the inner need for it – in fact, I regarded myself as an atheist for a short time, in rebellious mood! Experiences changed that, and much later, after some time in Subud, I was no longer content to remain outside the accepted mode of spiritual experience, and was confirmed in the Church of England.

It has since then seemed to me that my receiving through the Sacrament of communion is in source the same as in the latihan, the aspect of the intermediary being Jesus Christ in the case of Christian observance. It was the particular gentleness of the Sacrament which has soothed me at times when I have felt in danger of being thrown out of balance by surrender in the latihan.

It has been encouraging to have been close for a time to one or two Christians not in Subud. Their experiences of the purification and healing through Jesus Christ have enabled communication between us on a deep inner level.

MJ

The reality of Christ

In our South Devon group quite a few of us are committed Christians and I have noticed that all these come regularly to the latihan. For me the latihan has brought about a realisation of the inner content of Christianity. I feel a lot of people are groping for this.

I myself have had two experiences which have entered right into me. One morning when I was warden of Wisma Mulia (a Subud old people's home in Gloucestershire) I went up with another woman to have a latihan with Helen who was over 100 years old. After a little time I saw Jesus standing a few feet away in front of me. There was someone on either side of him, but I only saw the edge of their robes. He looked like no picture I have ever seen of him. But, 'How young he is!' was my immediate reaction, and, 'What vitality and strength!' He looked directly into my eyes and in his look was a content that has never left me. I have no idea how long he stood there. He was so real that I have no doubt he actually stood there.

Our house today is on the side of a hill overlooking the church and churchyard. One Christmas morning I was standing looking out of the window, wondering if I should go to the service later. It did not seem to matter one way or another. I began a latihan. After a few minutes I was aware very strongly of the presence of Christ in the corner of the room opposite me. Not his image, just his presence, radiating. The room began to fill with a radiant vibration that came from everywhere. It was in me and outside of me, in the corner with Christ. It came from outside and inside and filled all heaven and earth. And this radiance and vibration was God and came from God. It continued until the end of the latihan. The rest of the day was heaven on earth.

These two experiences of the reality of Christ entered right into me. Their validity was confirmed when I 'tested' in front of Bapak – not that I needed this confirmation truly. Subud has certainly made Christianity real for me. The reality is quite absolute, so having to have faith has nothing to do with it. It is like knowing your mother is your mother.

MW

Awareness of the Virgin Mary

As a child I was brought up without dogma between the Church of England of my father and the Russian Orthodox Church of my mother. By the age of twenty-one when I joined Subud (to please my husband-to-be who was already in Subud) I was a fairly regular churchgoer. However, it was only when I joined Subud that I had any sense of knowing God, of wonder or of joy.

I have had perhaps four major experiences in the Christian sense – and all concerned the Virgin Mary, of whom I was previously totally ignorant and had ignored. I will write of two of them.

The first was during a Subud weekend gathering in London. I was doing the latihan when I suddenly became aware of the Virgin

Mary beside me. How I 'knew' I really do not know, but there was no doubt. My eyes were shut so, of course, I did not see her in the normal sense. She was, however, a (dark blue) presence I could 'see'.

I did not mention my vision to anyone immediately, as I felt rather shy and overcome by it, but later, at lunch, I had a further experience. I was sitting with two friends who were coincidentally talking about Virgin Mary visions in Portugal and Yugoslavia. As I hesitantly started to describe my own experience that day, I was suddenly overcome by the sense of being enveloped by the Virgin's presence, and said in wonder, 'And she's here now, she's here now!' Again, there was no doubt. Tears of joy poured down my face. My friends shared my wonder.

I have never seen or felt the Virgin again in the same way, but I had one further experience concerning her about six months later. I was doing the latihan during Ramadhan in Indonesia and feeling sad that I no longer could see her. Then it occurred to me that I had no right to feel that way, and that I must include her in my life. At that moment I opened my eyes. Instead of seeing her with my own normal vision, everything was transformed. I saw love like something solid pertaining to everything and everyone around me. Between my inner self and the objects of my vision there was only Love. This state lasted the entire latihan. I kept opening my eyes to see with this wondrous sight, but my feelings of joy were mixed with the tears of realisation that I would have to return to my own cage, my cage where my vision was heavily filtered by my ego, my Self. It was exactly as though, as a prisoner in a windowless cell, I had been given the chance in a lifetime to look out at glorious freedom: another world.

Back to my cage I went, alas! but it seemed as though one or two veils had been lifted from my eyes and I became conscious from time to time of being able to see with love.

AA

Great good in the Catholic faith, but . . .

There was a time when I was receiving (as a convert to my husband's religion) so much in the Catholic mass that I felt drawn away from the latihan. This phase passed, however, and I now realise that it is only through the latihan that I have been able to receive so much from the Church. There are times in church when I feel I have to hold back from surrender in worship, and have to be very careful what I surrender to, because there are so many influences there. Yet I know for myself that, in spite of this, there is a very great good in the Catholic faith, and many good people in it. But there is sometimes a narrowness there, too, and a refusal to see that other religions also belong to God. But for us in Subud this is no problem.

MH

A Protestant deacon in Zaire

I am a confirmed Protestant Christian in Zaire. By the grace of God I have also found the way of Subud and have become a national helper.

During the years when we were isolated from the rest of Subud and there were divisions among us I did the latihan alone at home. It was necessary for me to go through a powerful experience. One day I felt my head touch the ceiling and my body expand larger than the room. I was afraid some power was interrupting the latihan, but was guided to continue. At the finish I felt my body all shrivelled up.

I wrote to a brother in France, a national helper, who told me not to be alarmed as this was a way in which impurities were leaving me. I must never cease to do the latihan, he said, which I have done to this day.

As to changes in my life, I used to be very nervous. For instance, when faced with a problem I used to go into a panic, but now I am always able to be calm inside. There has been a rebirth in both my life and in my religion through my many experiences.

I still go to church every Saturday or Sunday when I have time and exercise several functions, serving on the parish council and active as treasurer, and I continue to work as a deacon in my community.

NMR
[*Translated from the French*]

On being a Quaker in Subud

Quakers are enjoined to be 'open to new light from whatever quarter it may arise', and also to be alert to discern and interpret movements of thought and action in the world. This aspect of Quakerism is very congenial to me for, much as I love the Society of Friends, I feel that it ought to have more life and power, and that our meetings should make a more fruitful impact on the wider community. There are many people we seem unable to reach, and I joined Subud in order to see whether it offered another means of Grace through which God's Spirit could reach men. Isaac Pennington in 1666 warned us about using 'knowledge of truth declared in former ages' to withstand the present dispensations of truth. 'They may thereby,' he said, 'be hardened against that which should save them.'

What has my experience of the Subud latihan brought me?

First of all, there is an immediate influence on times of prayer, meditation and meeting for Worship. It now often happens that I pass without effort from the stillness of the body to inner stillness where the prayer of quiet is a reality.

To a remarkable extent the sense of frustration referred to above has been dissolved. I am aware of the limitations of my temperament and circumstances more sharply than before; but this awareness is accompanied by a strange contentment, a feeling that I am in my right place.

The Subud latihan has brought me experiences more profound than any in my life. In one there was a sense of God's Presence with me in such holiness that I was terrified and forgot my own name. Significantly enough (for I would call myself a Unitarian), the only thing I could murmur was, 'In the Name of the Father and of the Son and of the Holy Ghost.' Having said these words the glory seemed veiled so that I was back in myself and could pray and rejoice in it.

In the second I had an awareness that I was filled with hate – deep, impersonal hate which flowed over me like waves. This led to the facing of a dislike for one person which caused me much pain and distress until I was able to bring it to God and to make contact with a deeper level of myself. Almost at once this person was removed from my environment in circumstances that made her very happy.

The third experience was a knowledge that I am going to die. I mean by this a knowledge from the *inside* which I have never known before. All the things which I thought important seemed to unhook themselves and drift past me. There was nothing unhappy about this, and I was left with a curious feeling of *solidity*, as though something had been put into place.

It appears to me that through the Subud latihan there is a release of creative energy, and a way is opened for us to bring unaccepted and hidden aspects of ourselves into the light. As Robert Barcley found in the Quaker meetings; 'There is a secret power which touches the heart so that the evil in me was weakened and the good raised up.'

There are doubtless many ways to this experience, but although I am sure that God is always seeking to give His Spirit to men, there seem to be times and seasons when men are more receptive. At such times ordinary men and women – not only those who have prepared themselves by holy and dedicated lives – are able to draw on the springs of living water. This may be one such time, just as the beginning of Quakerism was another. As a Quaker historian wrote, 'Not only the rare spirits, but *all* were caught up into the new life.'

It is now three years since I began to follow the latihan. I am quite clear that, to use Bapak's own words, 'Subud is not a new religion, nor a sect of any religion, nor is it a teaching.' It is, I believe, a way of prayer that is helping me to understand religious truths inwardly, whereas before they had only been known to me as concepts. The greatness of God, His righteousness and judgment, are terms filled with new meaning. So, too, is the loving forgiveness of God, the sense of His Presence even when I am angry or frightened and in rebellion against Him.

To my surprise, I feel able to sympathise with points of view that hitherto have been anathema to me; even the words of evangelical hymns seem to contain a living message. Bapak has said that all Christians who follow the latihan must encounter the living Christ. I have not known this in any deep or catastrophic way, as did George Fox, but I find that I am becoming more tender towards to those who seemed to be narrowly Christocentric.

My difficulties and problems remain. I have no great achievements to report. But I can say two things: first, that through Subud God has become more real to me – and second, that Quakerism is confirmed as the right path for me as I try to worship and serve Him.

BC
[*written about 1965*]

Remaining true to Subud among the Charismatics

In 1982 our Scottish parish welcomed a new minister to replace the man who had left the year before. He was a warm, caring, humorous, well educated man, very open, and he and I immediately 'recognised' each other.

I had grown up in the Church but as I got older the 'big Daddy in the Sky' didn't seem real and I went the way of so many of us – atheist, eastern spiritual philosophy, and so on – until Subud. And Subud became my life.

So this lovely man entered our lives and I began to attend church. He spoke so beautifully, a true orator, so natural and real. I was very moved by it all and became quite active. In a village of 100 people, church life is important, and it became so for me. I went to Bible Study, had long talks with him, spoke of Subud, but became somewhat confused trying to understand how Subud and Christ's teachings could be compatible. In the 'inner' I could feel it, but to explain it was not easy.

Oh, there were still 'Sunday Christians' in that small body; there was pretence and hypocrisy. But for me that did not matter. I learned about atonement and prayer, and my heart was wrenched open many times.

Then we resettled in California. In my daily life I sometimes became very separated from my centre, the latihan. It was difficult to become quiet, especially when dealing with my two young boys. I felt the need for my heart to keep open, as it covered over and I became angry. Could Jesus help me?

I became friendly with C, the mother of a girl in my son's kindergarten class. She has an unusual quality, sensitive, deep, sincere, very real. We made a deep inner connection, not the usual response or experience I find with most people. A part of me is always looking for this deeper knowing with others. She is a born-again Christian and, as she knew I had been looking for a

Church, she recommended hers.

I told her of Subud, of my experiences, of my needs, of wanting to know Jesus more. But for her Jesus is 'the Way, the Truth and the Life'. Only through Him can God be reached. She is not the usual type of evangelical, and did not try to convert me in the traditional sense. But she cared for me, saw my sincerity. Her understanding is that Satan is working to keep people from Christ and God, and he can make things seem Godlike. To her the wonderful experiences we have in Subud and how our lives have changed are like that and keep us from Christ. The break between us was inevitable.

Knowing the Lord in Christ is very personal and sacred to me. Sometimes in church I find the openness of this gift of the spirit becomes too blatant and loses all fineness and subtlety. As to 'I am the Way . . .' I know He is, but not for everyone, as other ways suit other people. Sometimes I feel conflict, as I know that Christ would live in me more if I were more involved in the church in its fellowship, Bible Study, and so on. I am committed to Subud and that comes first.

I have thought about the latihan and the Holy Spirit and the gifts which the charismatics hold so dear. There is so much that blends, but who will listen? Few of my Subud friends are really interested, Christianity not being part of their spiritual experience. I dare not mention Subud to my Christian friends. As with C, I found they could not understand. The 'cultist' label is so inaccurate and hurtful. Having an unusual name sometimes raises suspicions.

So I get caught in the middle and am constantly having to surrender all that. I do what I can and am grateful for the addition to my life. I'm learning to feel comfortable with certain expressions like 'lifting up', but I avoid accepting Christian clichés simply in order to fit in. Besides conventional hymns, we also sing Songs of Praise, modern, beautiful, spirit-filled music which goes very deep and moves us all. Many people lift their arms as we might in the latihan. I do not feel comfortable in this, as I would be in latihan. But I am grateful to the addition in my life.

I do know that Christ lives and I have felt His presence and felt His Love which truly is unconditional. He bathes you in it. It is simply *there*. So much has become meaningful and clear.

HC

Subud and the rediscovery of the Holy Spirit in the churches

The pilgrimage which brought me, paradoxically, into both the Anglican ministry and Subud began when I found myself helpless to ease the suffering of a group of men with severe mental health problems. Searching for hope for the hopeless, those for whom all orthodox forms of treatment had failed, I began exploring other cultures. My goal was to escape from the stranglehold of the 'scientific' thinking current in the 1950s, which virtually reduced human beings to objects under the microscope, and to discover instead a new set of questions to ask and thus, I hoped, fresh answers.

What I discovered, as I looked eastward, was a holistic view of a human being, which had at its heart a spiritual dimension, one which stated very firmly that one looked inward not outward to discover the Truth.

The varied spiritual paths were united in claiming to be 'Ways of Liberation'. The questions I found myself asking were very simple. From what do they claim to be setting me free? Does it accord with my own experience, both personally and in what I see in the world around me? How can I be set free? And to what end? The answers were equally clear and to me rang true. What they indicated was that most of us were living our lives under the illusion that we were in control. Only rarely did we 'wake up' and glimpse the truth – that we were under the control of our passions, our prejudices and our drives, few of us ever coming close to fulfilling our human, let alone our divine, potential. It was when we recognised our helplessness to change ourselves, that there was a power, a force, the Spirit of God waiting in the wings, ready to work in us that process of purification which leads to the new freedom and quality of life called in the Bible 'Eternal Life'.

Tempted as I was by Eastern Philosophy, intellectual honesty necessitated that I take a fresh look at the 'dead' Christianity I had rejected in adolescence. There again was the same pattern. Adam, Man, depicted in the Genesis parable, as being at one with his Creator, having God's *ruach*, God's breath at work in him. Falling from grace through pride, he is immediately at the mercy of his passions – Cain and Abel, murder, greed, lust. Then, whatever happened through Jesus, the way was open again for man to experience God's Spirit. Suddenly the words of Paul, the Book of Acts, the promises of Jesus made sense. So too did the teachings of the Early Fathers, especially of the Eastern Church encapsulated in the *Philokalia* and St Simeon, the New Theologian. In these the twofold work of the Spirit was to act as the fire of purification and then of illumination, that we, too, might be lights to the world.

In 1964 I discovered Subud and felt right about it, but it was not then appropriate for me to be opened. To my surprise, and totally against my natural inclinations, by 1966 I found myself at a theological college training for the Anglican ministry, aware both of Subud and the rediscovery of the Holy Spirit in the Church as a living experience. A year later, again to my consternation, God made it clear I should enter Subud. Try explaining that to one's spiritual director in college! Why the latihan and not the specifically Christian experience of Baptism in the Holy Spirit, then manifesting itself rapidly in the mainstream churches, and, as a movement, finding perhaps its most balanced spiritual home in churches such as the Roman Catholic, that already had a long tradition of spirituality and discipline?

In the years that have followed in my ministry, the answer to that question has been given. While the latihan has continued to work in me inwardly, its guidance and the teaching of Bapak meant that I was able to be of help to my congregation and many others as they found themselves caught up in the charismatic renewal in the church, that renewal of the heart and mind that St Paul talks about. This was especially important when they encountered the 'crises' that such a working of the Spirit of God can produce as a necessary part of our spiritual growth. In teaching, in counselling, in preaching, in ways only half understood, I have sensed cause to be grateful for the grace of God in the latihan.

The dilemma, of course, for the Christian is the relationship of the power at work in the latihan to the Holy Spirit encountered through the Church. My own belief is that, qualitatively, and in the way in which their results are manifested in daily life, they are different. I am equally sure however, that both are ours through the grace of Almighty God and that the power of God at work through the latihan, with its ability to reveal to us the oneness of creation and the truth of God in other faiths, is very much God's gift for the future of mankind.

GC

At home with interchurch charismatic activity

I find that Subud has made my faith more and more real to me as I experience the wonderful Peace of God, the blessing of answered prayer and His guidance in my life. I have experienced the presence of Jesus and the Holy Spirit in church and in the latihan; and the Lord's Prayer sung in many different ways has often figured in my latihan too. I find I need both the latihan and the church. If I neglect either I get into trouble.

I feel I belong to the Christian community, not just the C of E kind. Three of the inner city churches – Methodist, United Reform and Catholic – in Chester (England) have been getting together, having joint services from time to time, starting projects and having conferences. Lately we have been inviting each other to attend our communion services. This, the central part of the Church's life, I feel is very important. I remember when I first took part in the new service, when we were offered 'The Body of Christ' and we had to answer 'Amen', I had a very strong sense of receiving. Later, in Scotland, I suddenly came to understand the other aspect of the 'Body' of Christ when we all shook hands when sharing the 'Peace of Christ'. I felt very strongly that we all were His hands, feet, eyes and ears in the world.

I came to understand the 'intercession of Mary' for us when I was in Scotland. I often found myself singing the first part of the Hail Mary in the latihan, and sometimes when I wake in hot sweats and pain I say the Hail Mary and receive a great sense of love and warmth, and the pain goes; I somehow get above it. Also when I was in Scotland I took part in a Catholic charismatic prayer group. I was delighted with it and easily fitted in. There is a C of E church here which is rather on those lines.

Lately I have been attending a Tezé interdenominational prayer-group held in the chapel of perpetual adoration. It was there, as we sang the beautiful chants, that I had several inner visions of Jesus.

AA

This is my bounden duty and service

Today I go to church in a Sussex village where I find among several of the Christian faithful a grace and warmth I did not encounter in the low church of Holland when I was young. This often seemed to provide only moral teaching, with often splendid ministers, to be taken on an either intellectual or emotional level. My only attraction was to the Roman church, where the Latin and the liturgy hid a mystery that could not be expressed by the ordinary mind. As Catholicism was taboo in my family, religion had no further appeal and life's hardly conscious search led through Ouspensky and John Bennett to Subud.

Twelve years ago I joined a Bible group led by my neighbours and in the readings noticed a life and understanding in the words inexplicable except through Subud's inner awakening. Then, on going to our beautiful old church one morning, there was a communion service and, almost as if by mistake, I went up to the rail and sensed the devotion of the people next to me. I felt this was the right service because it was not just a listening but an action, a bringing of yourself to the holy receiving.

I asked the priest whether he minded me coming to this service as a Dutch Protestant. He answered that he would never send anybody away, but advised me to be confirmed, which I did, and I have been to the early communion service on Sunday mornings ever since. Taking myself there bodily is a consciously willed act of witness – not to be in fantasy, but to meet Life, the Christ, the latihan bindingly. 'This my bounden duty and service', as the prayer after the Sacrament puts it. 'You in me and I in You.' It took about twenty years for Subud to bring me back to the Church.

AKR

A freedom from religion – so far

I was brought up in the Congregational Church, but the services meant little to me and I stopped attending as soon as I could. At the same time, I felt there must be comething meaningful to my inner life. The search for something real brought me into Subud, and I have found that the latihan and prayer have given me what I need, or at least what I am capable of taking on. I have had no feeling to adopt a formal religion, in spite of what Bapak has said about the desirability of doing so. In fact, it is true that I have felt a freedom from religion up until now. However, I have recently received indications that are pushing me gently towards the Christian faith.

HH

A priesthood fulfilled through Subud

I am a Colombian born in 1956, the eighth of fifteen children. After secondary school I entered the main Cathedral Seminary in Bogota and was ordained priest at the age of twenty-six. I worked for three years in parishes and then three more years as teacher and instructor in the main seminary. After much prayer and reflection I entered the Anglican Church in January 1988. In March of the same year I received the Subud opening in Bogota. In May I married Monica Ramirez, founder of the educational foundation, AMOR, where, for the last three years I have been engaged in social work. I also have a parish in a poor 'barrio' which I attend to at weekends.

On the subject of my priesthood, Subud and religion, I would like to say that before receiving the Catholic ordination I already knew a little about Subud through my older brother who has been a member for twenty years. But it was the guidance of God that led me to enter Subud. On the day of my opening I felt that I was again receiving the grace of the day of my ordination. From that moment I felt free of many ties that did not allow me to be happy, free to dedicate myself, as I am now doing, to work for others.

The latihan has strengthened my faith, my vocation and my sincere desire to give myself to others. For me now the mysteries and dogmas are no longer a problem and each day I am clearer about them. It has become very easy for me to understand and preach the work of God. Subud has been for me a complete opening from my inner towards the Divine. It has brought me to understand better the role of religions in the world, and is proof of the Oneness of God.

As a Christian, I feel Christ very much inside me, as well as the Holy Spirit. I am aware of my role within the Church and of my openness towards other Christian communities, as well as non-Christian communities – something that I didn't understand or accept before when I was tied to the closed structures and rules of the Church. Subud is for me like a road where all believers of different religions can meet, support each other and grow spiritually. What is important in any religion is the sincere surrender to God.

Now, more than ever, I am fulfilled and happy as a priest, as a social worker, as a husband, parent and Subud member.

You have asked me my view of the 'theology of liberation'. I have always thought that a true theology of liberation is based only the word of God and must not be subject to so many rules and structures that make it difficult for someone to serve others fully, as was done by the Prophets, by the Apostles and by Christ himself. I understand the theology of liberation to be that which feeds on the grace that springs from prayer and from the love of others.

O de los R
[Translated from the Spanish]

At holy communion

Where I live now I go most Sunday mornings to the ancient church at the top of the hill for the family Communion Service. It goes hand in hand with the most necessary sustenance of my twice or three times weekly latihans.

There have been Sundays when I have felt myself irked by 'sermons from the head', by people who whisper to each other and look around them, by hymns which are occasionally trite and laboured, and the recital of set prayers which often seem aimed at instructing the All Highest how to behave about this world. But always by the end of the Service I have realised that a point of real value was reached which made me glad I had gone. And it was always during the Communion Service.

More and more I see how, from the 'words of humble access', it has been beautifully devised so that gradually hearts and minds become stilled, until with the culminating chant of 'Grant us Thy Peace' there is a great hush and a great unity in which people's thoughts have momentarily dropped away from them. After the choir have received communion and the small children gone up to be blessed, the choir and congregation sing hymns, seated in their pews, as the people go row by row to the communion rail.

When my turn comes to kneel there, I feel as though in latihan, and am aware that my voice involuntarily responds in latihan, in a whisper, as I accept the wafer in my cupped hands and then sip from the chalice. And back in my seat I have a feeling of love and closeness as I look at the faces of those coming back down the aisle, most of them only known by sight.

On a very few occasions, when I have felt an initial reluctance to go to church and it didn't seem important to me to go, I have asked, 'tested', if it was indeed necessary for me to go. The answer has been such a light and joyous feeling of worship that I have gone along with quite a changed attitude. At other similar times when I have been disinclined to go and vaguely have in mind to test my attitude, I find that without pausing to do so, my hands are busying themselves about getting myself ready – and suddenly my coat and shoes are on and, just in time, I am out of the house and on my way as though propelled. Once when I did 'receive' to stay home, at the time I would have been in church there was a telephone call to ask me to go to someone who was sick.

So I begin to understand that it is indeed necessary, as Bapak has told us, for man to 'have a religion and follow it faithfully to the end of his days'. When I stayed with a member in Sussex last summer and we attended the parish church in Lewes, I felt great gladness when I looked around and saw several Subud members also in the congregation, one of them taking around the offertory plate. It is good to be joined with Subud sisters and brothers in this worship as well as having the deeper bond of our common worship in the latihan.

MS

Prayer, confession, fasting

My experience so far has been that people in Subud underestimate the meaning of religious practices, counting solely on latihan. My family and I are practising Catholics. We attend regularly the Sunday masses, celebrate traditional holidays, observe Lent. But it was not always like that.

Before being opened in Poland and for about two years afterwards, there was no religion in our family except the two traditional feasts, Christmas and Easter, and occasional chats about principles of our Christian faith. I would hear now and then that apart from latihan, religion was still important for us. But I thought that it was not necessary. I had the impression that religious practices were inferior to latihan.

Then more and more problems started to arise that I did not know how to solve without introducing religion into our life. Most pressing was a need for prayer. In prayer I could focus on my little or big problems and ask God for help. I could explain prayers to our children: how they can express their gratitude, how they can ask for forgiveness, for help, and how they can worship God.

Then there were countless questions from our children about the meaning of different things they had imagined or heard about. First I tried to answer from my couple of years' experience in latihan but it was not clear to me, even less to children. And at the same time our religion had given us centuries of practice, of explanations, thousands of illustrative stories. So I drew all those treasures from the Bible, and it worked quite well.

Another thing was confession. Once, just before leaving our refugee hotel in Austria to come to Canada, we found ourselves in a critical family situation. It often happens that when you most need testing you rarely ask for it. The problem is too personal or you do not feel like talking to helpers about it. From my childhood in Poland I remembered the refreshing feeling of immediate purification after a confession. I felt that now, once again, the confession could give me new strength and clarity. Afterwards I felt that at least my part of the mess had been cleared. But there was more to it than that: a nucleus of truth and strength from chaos arose and started to be the basis for a new family life.

Another thing was fasting. When I did Ramadhan together with others in my first years in Subud, it was always full of events of

95

deep meaning. Nights of Power spent together with some Subud brothers and sisters, and Bapak's talks – that was a wonderful experience. But I felt separated from my family. The children did not understand and my wife did not share the feeling. She used to say, 'Ramadhan is not our culture, is not our tradition; it's strange and foreign to me . . .'.

So I started to do both: Lent with my family and Ramadhan with the Subud family. But it was too much, too strong. One helper told me that I should not be greedy. Now we observe Lent with my entire family. Each of us chooses individually the constraints we are able to stand. This makes us much closer to each other.

Religion has a firm place now in our family life and I confirm with my strong experience the truth of Bapak's words about the need for it as well as the latihan.

JP

Pain of being dismissed as a cultist

My search led me in many directions – other religions, drugs, and occasionally back to church. Then, on a trip to Ottawa, I met L, my husband (it was one of those experiences you read about – I knew him immediately, and that he would be my life partner) and when he told me about Subud, I went for the whole package! But much to my dismay, my new-found love did not experience that same revelation as I did – he insisted that he wasn't looking for a girlfriend, that at the age of twenty-four he wanted a wife and family. I was happy to oblige, but he thought I was too young. It took almost a year, during which time I went through a very condensed growing-up process, before L asked me to marry him. I was opened two weeks later. I was seventeen.

We were married in Ottawa in the Anglican Church, and we even taught Sunday school for a while. When our first child was born we invited a Subud couple to be her godparents. They were very happy to travel the 200 miles for the Baptism, but what they did not expect, nor did we, was the lecture we received from the pulpit that day. We had told our pastor about Subud, not in any attempt to 'convert' anyone, but because we felt that if we were entrusted with teaching the children of the congregation, we should have no secrets from the rector.

Somehow he misunderstood what we had shared with him. He gave a sermon on 'cults and instant spiritual gratification'. We were hurt and embarrassed. We never even tried to set the record straight; I guess we both felt so new and inexperienced in Subud, we weren't sure we wouldn't make matters worse. So except for a few midnight Masses at Christmas, we never went back. My other two children have never been baptised. And on the odd occasion when I did return to church, I would look at the Apostle's Creed and say to myself, 'I can't say that – I'm not sure that I believe it.' I prayed for years that I would receive the content of my religion. I continued my latihan confident with the idea that this was enough.

The writer finally understood that this was not so, and she returned to church and received the Anglican confirmation. Through the caring and instruction of a priest, Father E, she was led through all doubts into the heart of her faith and into religious studies.

At first I was unsure of how I would react to theology, fearing my 'natural spirituality' would be crushed by rigid dogma and hard doctrine. I have discovered instead to my delight that theology is the study of endless possibilities. The university I attend is basically Roman Catholic, with mostly religious professors (priests and nuns). I was and am continually amazed and pleasantly surprised by the forward thinking and openness, sometimes the bold courage, I am encountering in my studies. I sense a new maturity, a new consciousness here, a renewed respect for the Power of God; recognition that there is no ownership or exclusivity with God's forgiveness and blessing; that yes, there is salvation outside the church; a new respect and awareness of the integrity of indigenous peoples, religions and cultures, and that although the missions continue, the missionaries are now encouraged to find God as He/She already exists, to find Christ as he already exists, within the life and culture and religion of others.

I remember reading that Bapak said that our most important task in life is to remind others to worship, to commune with God (he didn't say bring them to Subud), because God reveals Godself to each one of us in God's own way, and is constantly there. We need only remind others to listen – and we each listen best in the language, symbols, culture, and so on, which is closest to our own nature.

RC

A Hungarian explores deep waters

I was born in Hungary in 1945 and lived in Budapest. Hungary has a strong mystical tradition based on Hinduism and Buddhism and Hungarian scholars have translated and written commentaries on the sacred texts. I discovered my father had a big library of books on yoga and philosophy; also a friend who was a hatha yoga master taught me exercises to control various physical functions. At the same time I was very interested in swimming and diving. I was in three national teams and also became scuba diving champion of Hungary. In part this was related to an interest in physical discipline, but it had another aspect too, which was searching for the unknown adventure, the mystical depth. We went down into the deep waters of lakes and wells and caves where visibility was poor. There was the idea of going deep, of searching for some kind of spiritual treasure.

In 1964 when I was nineteen I left Hungary. My aim was very specific. I hoped to find my wife, my spiritual master, and adventure. I was sure I was going to 'make it rich, real quick' and then I could bring my family out. I went first to France where I was granted political asylum. I worked in a secondary school and at the same time I was able to prepare for the school examination. During this time I got to know a group of people who were interested in Gurdjieff and this was a lead-up to my coming into Subud later on. I tried to enter medical school, but didn't succeed; then I got a visa to go to the United States in late 1966. The social worker who was assigned to help me with settling in was a Subud member. She noticed on my paperwork my interest in hatha yoga, and we started talking about spiritual things and she mentioned Subud.

And as soon as I heard it, I knew. 'That's it!' I had no questions. It was so clear to me. At the Subud house in New York there was a vibrant atmosphere and the second person I talked to was Hungarian. I spent my waiting period at his place, sipping coffee and talking about everything except Subud. I had no questions, and so we discussed our life and adventures and eventually I was opened.

I was fortunate enough to obtain a full university scholarship to Yale, where I first studied pre-med but then changed to economics and business administration. I made some money on the side teaching hatha yoga. Some of my pupils came into Subud. When I finished at Yale I was accepted at the Harvard Business School and completed a master's degree in business administration. My expectations were built up very high. I had listened to Bapak's advice about enterprises, and I wanted to do my own business but it was a difficult time – the oil crisis and so on – and my first efforts were not successful. Then I went through a period of very heavy purification and ran rather wild for a couple of years.

This came to an abrupt end in 1975 when my mother died. My mother's death made me ask myself what I was doing with my life. I felt like the prodigal son who had wasted all his opportunities. A month after her funeral the Hungarian authorities gave me a visa, for the first time in ten years. It was then that I had one of my biggest Subud experiences.

Late one afternoon I went into a church on the Avenue of the Martyrs in Budapest. I just stepped in. It was the kind of thing my father used to do. He would say, 'Well, let's just go in for a "sigh" '. So I went in for a 'sigh'. There were many people inside, a feeling of deep worship, deep silence, and I just surrendered all of a sudden to God and asked: 'Well, here I am, what can I do?' And it was as if a door opened into the other world and Christ was standing before me. He was completely real, he was alive, three-dimensional. I could even see him breathing. His body and his white robe were transparent, just like in the holy pictures, and I could see his burning heart. I felt it was this energy coming from his heart that had opened the door and that kept us alive. It lasted for only a few seconds, but it changed my life.

IG

A Visit to Fatima

I had been brought up a Catholic, so I was well aware of the story of Fatima in Portugal, how the Virgin Mary appeared a number of times to three peasant children in 1917, bringing them various experiences, messages and prophecies. But in adolescence I had drifted away from the church and it was only when I found Subud that I was again open to believing in something like Fatima.

I went to Fatima one February. It was a good time to be there, the end of winter. The nights were cold, the days warm and sunny. There were very few pilgrims. In the centre of Fatima is a vast square with a basilica and a chapel which marks the spot where the Virgin appeared. Half a mile from this sanctuary a path goes off into the fields to the place where the children had two visions of the Angel in 1916. It is very peaceful here and you can imagine yourself in the world the children inhabited.

Each day in Fatima I went to the sanctuary to mass and communion, then walked up into the hills where the Angel appeared. I read from the memoirs of Lucia, one of the children.

Within hours of being there I felt my distress fall away. I can compare it to the experience of doing Ramadhan in Cilandak. There was a palpable atmosphere, such a feeling of peace. It was like the reassurance that comes from a mother.

I felt a detachment from the clamour and seduction of the material world in a deeper way than I had previously experienced. I could see the difference between everything that belongs to this world, the material world, and what belongs to the other world, the world of grace, of God's power, the supernatural world from which Mary came to make her appearances. It was as if Fatima was an opening in the material world through which grace could flow from the other world.

I arrived in Fatima on Wednesday night and by Saturday I knew it was time to go. Part of me could have stayed there forever, but I knew that I had now received the essence of what was necessary.

On Saturday I went to the basilica in the morning as usual, to mass and communion, and walked up into the hills where the Angel had appeared. Around three o'clock in the afternoon I went down to the bus station to wait for the bus. There were some souvenir shops at the station and at one of them I bought a cassette tape of Fado, the Moorish influenced folk music of Portugal. I put the tape into my portable cassette player and, with the first few notes of the music, sweet, sensual and melancholy, the material world came flooding back into me. It was only at that moment as it came flooding back that I realised how empty I had been.

Back came the clamour and seduction, the sweetness of the material world, its sensuality and its inevitable sadness. I was back on the wheel of suffering and desire. Strangely, this most Catholic of experiences seemed to present itself in Buddhist terms.

The visit to Fatima also made me more open to Islam. It is strange that an experience so Catholic should have made Islam more accessible, that the experience of Fatima which has so much to do with pity, compassion, a mother's love and intercession, should have made it possible for me to accept the uncompromising quality of the Koran, but it was so.

Christianity and Islam, compassion and commitment, they are not opposites, but like opposite sides of the same coin. The deeper you go into one, the closer you come to the other.

When I returned from Portugal I went on a retreat to a Carmelite monastery near Oxford. I was able to follow the monks in their round of prayer and this helped establish the beginnings of a discipline of religious observance in me. My last day at the monastery was Ash Wednesday. I rose for mass with the monks in the chapel at 6.30 am. Snow was falling softly outside as the darkness lifted. One of the monks asked me if I would read the lesson. Then I joined the procession of monks to have my forehead marked with ashes – ancient ritual, so familiar from childhood. So I began my observance of the season of Lent.

HS

This account may stand for others not printed here, on the meaningfulness and consequences of pilgrimages to Fatima, Medjugorje, and other Christian shrines and sacred places.

Back to Judaism – with enjoyment

When I first joined Subud I had no time for religion. Indeed, anything which smacked of a religious attitude or terminology got my back up immediately, even the name of God. I had long ago rejected Jewish practices and observances. Gradually, however, my attitudes changed. After a year or two I could use the word 'God', and my experiences little by little started to build a belief in the existence of God.

Later I started to feel the need to pray and at first did this without words, and then with my own personal prayers. Then I felt the need for a religion, translating this into a feeling of duty. I became more Jewish than I had been as a child, observing more of the dietary laws than we had even done at home. At this time I was quite puritanical in other ways as well. I would not see violent or sexual films and totally avoided alcohol. I also avoided any sexual involvement, although very much wanting to marry.

At this time I had a dream in which I was walking in the crypt of an old building, with the roof and arches so low that I banged my head when I walked in a half-crawling position. I tested this dream with the helpers and it appeared to be an indication that the path I was following was contrary to my nature.

After this I abandoned religion for a while, but have now returned to what seems to be a more natural way for me. I returned a second time to my religion with a feeling of relief that I could enjoy again what had given me pleasure as a child. I enjoy going to synagogue occasionally and spending all Saturday morning feeling the quiet enjoyment of the worship through the music of the service.

This last Yom Kippur, for the first time I felt the reality of my sins being forgiven and a wonderful feeling of lightness and refreshment, accompanied by the latihan.

I feel this too sometimes after morning prayer. I often find that I wake up between 4 and 5am and that, if I wash and say my prayers, I go back to bed so fresh and at peace that I have a totally refreshing sleep until 7am. But, if I sleep straight through the night, I'm just as happy to say my prayers then.

My whole lifestyle has relaxed over the last few years and I now enjoy a drink with friends and can see many types of films without them upsetting me.

Recently I got married. My wife feels Muslim and testing has shown that for her it is better that she remains inwardly Muslim while outwardly enjoying Jewish customs and traditions. We both feel very happy about this.

We had a Jewish wedding ceremony conducted by a Subud member with the advice and permission of his (Reform) Rabbi. We have been to synagogue together several times and enjoyed a Seder (Passover) meal with some friends last Easter. Recently my wife suggested we observe a Friday night ceremony to welcome in the Sabbath. We look forward to doing this and many other Jewish things together and, if God wills, with our children.

SB

Christ as regulator of a Muslim's Grace

I was brought up as a Christian but educated in multi-racial schools in the Far East so have always been used to the cultures of many different religions.

After I married, I knew it was right I should become a Muslim, join the same religion to which my husband had converted. He is also in Subud. At first I felt this to be a terrible betrayal of my own Christian religion. But gradually I came to experience that this was not so, as I began to appreciate the unity of the source of both religions through my latihans . . .

One evening recently, the first day of Ramadhan, before I started my latihan with the group, I prayed privately for spiritual help. I had been through a particularly gruelling time when I had been burdened with heavy worldly problems and responsibilities. I asked for grace to help me cope with these pressures in my life.

In this latihan I found myself able to surrender so deeply I reached a point where I could not bear to receive any more grace. I felt I had reached the end of my capacity to surrender. But the latihan continued and I suddenly found myself in a different place, although I knew my body was still in the latihan room. This other place was completely filled with light in which I gradually realised Christ was present. It was so bright I could scarcely stand it, and felt myself 'drowning in the Glory of God' – this is the only way I can describe it.

I began to panic, but at that moment I realised the amount of grace I was being allowed to receive and experience was in some way being regulated by Christ. In this moment I suddenly understood the meaning, for me, of Christ the Saviour. He seemed to be saving me from totally drowning in grace, somehow controlling the situation. I heard myself repeating 'Saviour, Christ the Saviour' and then came back to my normal state.

I don't pretend to understand this experience fully. But I do feel it has helped me to feel closer to the Christians I do meet, within and outside Subud. Meanwhile I continue to practise Islam to the best of my limited ability.

RD

A Muslim helps a Christian into his faith

By 1971, belief in God had not as yet led me back to Christianity. At the Subud World Congress in Jakarta I took a personal problem to Mas Darto, a Muslim helper. To my astonishment he used a term that Islam rejects: son of God. He advised me that by surrendering the problem to God through the latihan – as it was something inherited (he said) through my father (God bless him) – I would gradually lose the problem and, in a spiritual sense, cease to be a son of an earthly father, and become a son of God.

Did Mas Darto know I would one day become a Christian? He left unsaid the logical implication: that being purified of one's sins means becoming a son of God ('Our Father, who art in Heaven') – whether you are a Christian, a Muslim, or whatever – and that the only man totally free from sin can be called the son of God. I now realise this provides a logical reason for the doctrine of the Virgin Birth (no inherited sins), which also links to the doctrine of the Redemption (Christ having no sins in Himself to suffer for). 'No one comes to the Father save through Me.' We come to God through gradually becoming what Jesus is – son of God – by being purged of our sins.

Well, it took me many years to work all that out, greatly helped by the Christian writings of CS Lewis. In *The Great Divorce* he has a story of a man purified of a particular sin symbolised by a lizard turning into a horse on which the man then rides away. It was crucial for me.

A Christian needs a Church as the latihan needs Subud. At last at Epiphany, 1979, I was received into the Roman Catholic Church.

RH

Born-again Muslim

I am a 'born again Muslim', a good term to describe my experience. From being a devout – or, rather indoctrinated – Muslim up to mid-teens, I gradually progressed to total atheism until my rebirth in Islam via Subud. I am a Muslim in the Bapak mould and not a fundamentalist in the sense that this term is normally understood.

I do consider myself, however, a fundamentalist in the sense that I accept without reservation that the Quran is the World of God as conveyed to the Prophet. This is a totally different concept from the inspired writings of saintly men.

Further, I hold the view that the Quran is couched in language which renders its essential message valid for all time and for all peoples. It follows that the external manifestation of Islam – the way of life of its followers and the observance of religious injunctions – is not fixed and must vary, having regard to different time periods, geographical areas and racial and cultural factors.

For me, the latihan is a gift from God which we receive two or three times a week and with which we cannot, or ought not to, interfere. Our worship of God, on the other hand, is expressed through our actions and is not something which is limited to two or three times a week. Hence, as a Muslim I consider it necessary to follow the Islamic way of saying five prayers spread out during a day, reciting and reading the Quran (in translation) and fasting during Ramadhan. All this helps perpetuate 'fear' of God – fear in the sense that a decent and well-behaved child fears his parents. Such remembrance and fear lead to stirrings of wisdom which is distinct from the cleverness of mind.

SA

How I became a devout Muslim in Subud

I was born to a Muslim Turkish family in Cyprus in the year 1926. My family had great respect for religion but they were not practising it strictly except for fasting during Ramadhan. I was therefore accustomed to fasting but not doing anything else. Although it was against Islam I liked drinking in my youth.

At the age of twenty-four I started attending lectures on Gurdjieff. This aroused in me a great interest towards the esoteric and mystical side of religion. I started research on various faiths and my attention was turned to people who worked on themselves for spiritual perfection. But this came to a climax only when I discovered Subud in 1957 through Husein Rofé, who was then teaching in Cyprus.

After being opened by Bapak in London in June 1957 I had formed the view that Subud was the gist of religion and nothing else was required, feeling a bit proud also that I had started receiving and feeling things which put me to the right path. But in the meantime my belief in the orthodox side of Islam started to grow and a year later I decided to go on pilgrimage to Mecca, where I had the greatest experience in my life. I was doing my Muslim prayers on Mount Arafat and asked, as is the habit before the end of the day, whether my pilgrimage was accepted by God and my sins pardoned. I received that I was entering a house. There I saw Bapak standing inside the hall and introducing people whose pilgrimage was accepted to Prophet Muhammed s.a. who was sitting on a divan and whose face was all light. Then I formed the view that for me the way to the Prophet was through Bapak and I thanked God for being in Subud and for being accepted to the presence of the Prophet. This was a proof to me that I should practice the orthodox side of the religion as well, and thus complete the circle, as the one was connected with the other and neither could become complete without the other.

Later on I started living my religion fully, while not neglecting my latihan – as some people in Subud did and left Subud by saying that they had found what they wanted. (In Cyprus we have two old Subud members who left Subud and became imams in mosques). I now obey fully the five pillars of Islam by believing that God is one and Muhammed s.a. is his last messenger, by fasting, by praying five times a day, by giving one fortieth of my income as alms and by having visited Mecca once in my lifetime (my financial position having allowed me to do so).

I soon discovered that my attitude had drawn the attention of people around me who became more respectful towards me and found me more sincere and a good believer in God. During this time my interest and respect in other religions increased day by day and I found out that the stronger I was in my religion, Islam, the stronger was my respect in other religions. When once I went to visit the Greek Orthodox monastery of St Barnabas in North Cyprus the three monks there, who were by coincidence brothers, said to me; 'You look like an official of the Archbishopric rather than a Muslim'. This reminded me of the poet Rumi who said that there is no difference between the religions, which are like taps from a water tank taking their water from the same source. Men do not open the taps to see that the water flowing from them is the same and they fight with each other for the colour or the name of the tap, not knowing the content. I therefore thank God for making me a devout Muslim through Subud and a respectful person among the congregation of mosques and an international person at any prayer place.

HF

Testimony of a Shi'ite woman

I was born in Sierra Leone and am of the Lebanese Shi'ite Muslim faith. While my mother's family can be considered rigid, even fanatical, my father's people were more enlightened and accepted their Christian neighbours as equals. In fact, my whole education from elementary to high school to university was Christian based. I admired Christianity very much and remained a good Christian at heart but I dared not openly go forward and ask to be baptised. After my O Levels my parents refused to let me go for further studies. I spent two frustrating years at home. My whole heart was set on continuing my studies because to me education meant and still means freedom and achievement, self-actualisation and self-fulfillment – a special kind of happiness. During this time I was taught the Islamic prayers by my brother Nassir.

One night I was praying very late, *Salat almughreb* and *Salat alishaq* (the evening and night prayers), when I heard someone call my name, *Manar!* I jumped up and ran to my parents but they were already sleeping. The story of the call of Samuel came to me. I went back to my prayer mat to continue my prayers. The voice came back to me – *Manar, Manar, Manar!* So I said what Samuel said: speak, for thy servant heareth! Then the answer came through my own mouth: God is hearing and accepting your prayers! This happened when I was still in Sierra Leone with my family. Soon afterwards they approved my going to Lebanon to continue my studies.

In Lebanon I searched in many movements for something that validates all. I also included Bible studies in my courses. But all these left me dissatisfied and still thirsty. In my first year philosophy courses I drifted far from my former fervent religiousness. I neglected my prayers and Ramadhan. I became very hard inside and put a barrier between myself and others. I became indifferent.

Then I joined Subud and at last found the depth and inner meaning I was looking for. I felt my senses opened and have experienced the submission that most Muslims only preach about and do mechanically as instructed.

I was enabled to develop my own outlook on life. As Shi'ites or any seekers of God we should be our true natural selves in our worship of Almighty God, not copy anyone else. I cannot help seeing a great many Muslims today reverting to and imitating the past. This planned and organised submission is done with the heart and mind and, I think, it limits us and prevents the higher forces developing us.

Through the latihan I have come to recognise every human being as a creation of God, like myself. What right have I, therefore, to judge others as, for instance, the Sunni and Shia do, largely for political reasons, instead of following the way of tolerance taught by the Prophet Mohammad?

Through Subud the inner darkness has been lifted, my heart has opened and my pure feelings have become alive once more. I find it easier to worship the One Almighty God – Allah Akbar, the true essence of Islam – which itself means submission to Almighty God. A very special feeling arises in my inner for my Muslim prayers and whenever I hear the Holy Quran being recited. I feel I love all religions and I am not ashamed to stand and tell anybody who asks that I am a Muslim and a Shi'ite too, but that I owe it all to my submission and purification through the latihan of Subud.

DMR

At home in both mosque and church

One year after joining Subud I was working in Beirut, and was impressed by how my fellow Subud members, who were Armenian and Greek, sincerely followed the five daily prayers of Islam, the Ramadhan fast and also fasting on Mondays and Thursdays. They did this at the risk of becoming outcasts in their own communities.

For the next Ramadhan I learned the Muslim prayers without considering myself a Muslim. Two years later, after daily practice of the prayers and fasting, I embraced Islam in Bapak's presence in Cilandak. When he asked me why I was becoming a Muslim I replied that I believed Islam includes all other religions and Bapak said loudly, 'Good, good!'

That was sixteen years ago. Since returning to England three years ago and settling in Bedford I have started a Friday evening Koranic study group attended by local Muslims. But a deeper contact with Muslims not in Subud is difficult because of their rigid attitude of mind. When my views of what is the spirit of the Holy Koran rather than the literal word provoke argument I keep quiet to avoid being 'put straight' by traditional Muslims.

Subud is not a religion but for me Bapak's talks are often more appropriate to our needs today, more relevant to the age we live in. Subud is the centre of my life and participation in Subud activities – I am at present regional chairman – makes very secondary any joining in the life of the Muslim community. While the true spirit of Islam is identical to that of Subud, I am sometimes unsympathetic to what is practised or spoken in the name of Islam. For instance, not long ago the mosque in Bedford hosted a delegation of evangelical preachers, or *tabliq*, from London. They said quite literally that Islam is dying, at least in the UK, and blamed Muslims for neglecting their daily prayers in spite of the fact that Allah gives a certificate or diploma to every Muslim when he or she goes to the next world, inscribed with the number of daily prayers in the account. I cannot see Islam like this.

I am aware of the Power of Almighty God when I pray, regardless of whether my prayer is at home, in a mosque or in a church. The Prophet Mohammad compared God to a city. The religions are the various roads leading to that city and I do not believe that God has blessed one more than another. I do not feel different in a mosque to how I feel in church. I am equally at home in both. This convergence is, I believe, part of the harmony that Subud is bringing into the world, or has come to bring into the world.

RRR

A Japanese Buddhist's long road into Islam

If I look back over my Subud life, I remember two experiences or happenings which brought about radical changes to my relationship with religion.

I was brought up in a Buddhistic tradition and in my childhood was often taken to the temple. When I was still a pupil in primary school, my parents joined a new spiritual movement called Seicho-no-Ie which means Home of Growth. The founder is the late Dr Taniguchi, and it has several hundred thousand followers. He taught that we are all sons of God and all religions are in essence the same. He also taught that our situation is a reflection of our mind. His teaching caused many miraculous cures from illnesses among his followers, my mother being one of those cured. I worked for the publisher who was spreading this new 'gospel', but I was not totally satisfied with his teaching and was seeking something deeper.

In 1954 Husein Rofé came to Tokyo and I was opened among the first Japanese members. After a few years' practice of the latihan, I started having a recurring dream about shoes. I kept on losing my shoes, or they were the wrong size so that I could not go out in them. As it continued for several months, I wondered very much what this dream could mean. I knew Freud's interpretation about shoes [as a sexual fetish – Ed.], but didn't feel that it could explain my dreams.

Then, suddenly, one day I felt as though illuminated with a new understanding and realised that these dreams symbolised my relation with religion so far; shoes represented my religious concepts, with which I see and interpret in this world. Shoes are to protect our feet from touching the earth. I had been using my religious belief as a screen to protect myself from a direct contact with this harsh and irrational world, for I had been scared to face reality. The dreams indicated that this was not right and that since I had the latihan I should be really open to everything in the world, and should see, touch and accept the world as it is, like a newborn baby, without any preconceived idea or interpretation, and should have the courage to walk the earth, so to speak naked.

After this experience I ceased to have the dream of shoes and felt that I would not need religious faith or religious concepts any more, as latihan alone would suffice.

Then after some fifteen years in Subud, I had another experience. I had felt drawn to Islam for a long time and suspected that my inner faith would be Islam, but I hated the idea of embracing Islam outwardly. I didn't feel the need to have a religion and was just satisfied with the latihans. Moreover, in Japan, Islam was regarded as a peculiar religion and was known by most people at that time only by its practices of plural marriages and circumcision.

Then, one day, when I was walking with a Subud friend after group latihan, talking about the custom of circumcision in Islam, I felt again as though illuminated and, as I looked into myself, I saw myself as if walking on the street naked, without wearing any clothes. This lasted only for one or two seconds. I realised that for us who live in this world, inner reality cannot be complete until it has its outer expression or counterpart, and that I should have a religious practice with an outer form to follow, a *shariat*, the clothes representing my outer religion. I embraced Islam soon afterwards.

RT

The writer is currently chairman of the International Subud Committee.

No more needle in a haystack

The latihan entered my life at a time when I needed some direction. I came to Subud with an Islamic background. Even so, the latihan together with Bapak's talks have brought a new understanding, enabling me to see with greater clarity what in Islam is revelation and receiving, as opposed to all human interpretations which attempt to hide behind that label. For the truth in every religion is mixed up with ideas inherited from human interpretations not free from self-interest. In my search for what is essential for me in my religion the latihan has illuminated my path. Without it I would be looking for a needle in a haystack.

It is obvious that the message of Islam stems from the Koran and the example of the Prophet Muhammad. However, before coming to Subud, in my desire for esoteric knowledge I came across a certain sect which has constructed its own doctrine, investing particular individuals with absolute authority and divine status. These individuals claim to be saviours of souls, with powers to forgive sins and grant paradise in exchange for monetary dues, total devotion, and submission and obedience to their commands. The power exercised by these gurus is such that adepts cannot liberate themselves from their stranglehold without upsetting their lives. I was suffocating under this situation when I discovered Subud. However, it then took nearly three years to smash all the idols set up during the course of my association with these so-called esoteric teachings.

In 1983 I wrote to Bapak asking for some clarification about the maze of doctrines which are generated to legitimise institutional authority, and also the validity of the teachings of this sect and the claims of its leader. I quote part of Bapak's reply:

> Religion is a belief where the followers have faith in the dissemina-
> tion of the teachings which are respected in a particular religion.
> If you question whether all the teachings are true or not, Bapak
> can only say that the One Who knows the truth is only the One
> Almighty God. Regarding the *latihan kejiwaan*, to some extent
> you will experience spiritual realities, so that you will be aware,
> with conviction, of what is necessary to follow and carry out, and
> of what is unnecessary.

At first I was a little disappointed at this reply as Bapak did not directly answer my particular questions. Quite soon, however, my circumstances of life changed, so that I was brought into contact with a certain important *shaykh*. In the course of our conversation he felt that he should disclose to me that the esoteric leader in question had approached him in despair, begging for his spiritual help and guidance. This, and a series of other experiences, demystified for me completely the sanctity which I had imagined to surround this man and his teachings. Thereafter I felt liberated from all false doctrines that could prevent me from worshipping the One Almighty God.

'Salahuddin'

Challenge of Subud as a 'new paradigm'

I fully accept what Bapak says about the four stages of worship which encompass each other. The first stage, the *shariat*, consisting of religious observance without questioning, is the outer form of Islamic or, for that matter, any religious practice. For me the current fundamentalist versus modernist quarrel in Islam is at this stage and represents different ways of interpreting the Shariat in this day and age.

Above the *shariat* we enter into the realm of *tarekat*, characterised by the study of the inner content of religion. The Sufi traditions are the best Islamic example of *tarekat*. Beyond this, we reach the *hakekat*, the stage where the reality of religion is experienced (which, in Christianity, is usually termed grace).

Bapak tells us that the latihan of Subud is at this level of *hakekat*, where we may experience directly the essence or source of all religions. As this source is unique it becomes possible for individuals of different religions to receive the latihan together. The differences are simply transcended, each receiving according to his or her inner nature, even if that receiving is then interpreted through different religious or cultural lenses.

Still further is the stage of *mahrifat*, which is characterised by continuous receiving through God's grace. The *mahrifat* is in fact the manifestation of the reality of hakekat. Christ walking on the waters or curing the sick or the miraculous victory of Mohammed at Badr are signs (*muhjisat*) of this manifestation of *hakekat*.

Therefore, what is challenging for me as a Muslim in Subud is not to look back or get caught up in meaningless quarrels between fundamentalist and modernist, but that we should manifest first in ourselves and, I hope, in the world at large, a new reality, a new model or paradigm that will not only make obsolete division within Islam, but also between all religions and, for that matter, even between religious and non-religious observances. Subud is for me this new paradigm which cannot be measured or understood in terms of any former paradigm. It is the equivalent of a quantum leap in physics.

Viewed from this perspective, the Iran-Iraq war or a religious quarrel like that in Northern Ireland are maybe only the consequences or manifestations of a new spiritual paradigm in the world today. This new spiritual dimension is illustrated not only in Subud but in parts of what is called the 'new age' movement.

The positive result of these wars and sufferings is thus to accelerate the rise of a new consciousness, or realisation, that fanaticism is not the solution, because neither side has the truth but only a different shadow of the same truth – indeed, crystallised forms of what at their origin was a unique truth experienced at *hakekat* level.

If it is possible to re-experience that *hakekat* here and now, what, then, is the use of defending 'dead' truths? That is the challenge, as I see it.

This model of a new paradigm replacing an old one and causing immense suffering in order to reach a new consciousness has many parallels in history. The latest example was the need to go through the horrors of two world wars in order to realise that wars are really not the way. Now that same Europe of division and hatred has given place to a new European idea based on interdependence and peace. Can it be that what happened in Europe less than half a century ago is at work now in front of our eyes, but this time on a world-wide scale?

RJ

How a Franciscan priest became head of the charitable wing of Subud

Wilbert Verheyen tells his story

In 1952 my training was over and I left Holland for New Guinea as a Franciscan priest. It was one of my ideals to work there, and my superiors gave me leave to go. I was soon made director of a complex of schools, and in 1955 I was sent to a parish.

In 1958 the Dutch Government opened up a new area called the Highlands of New Guinea. As always in New Guinea, there was competition between the Protestants and the Catholics. The Bishop of Jakarta, who knew about the government plans for the Highlands, said to us, 'I want you to go up there and work in the field of pacification, community development and afterwards of christianisation.'

All the tribes were very primitive, still in the Stone Age. They were in constant tribal warfare with each other and very isolated from anyone else. Our task was to explore the land, find out how many tribes there were and who were the chiefs, and afterwards do a kind of community development plan. We and the Protestant missionaries divided up the region of the Baliem Valley between us.

In the beginning I had a colleague. Neither of us were at all experts in anthropology, though we had lessons in it, but afterwards a linguist came up to help us with the language, and an anthropologist. Some members of the Harvard Peabody Expedition were also of real help.

The early work was mainly pacification – going to the chiefs, and making the first map of the valley, which took until about 1961. The first years were very interesting but also very difficult and rather dangerous years. A boy was murdered behind me on one of my journeys, and so was one of our teachers who was building his school. To try and eliminate me, one group held me for a month in a primitive prison with almost no food.

Humble about my own culture

But I'm always glad that I went through that experience as it made me rather humble about my own culture. I set out as a bringer of a new culture, a bringer of peace and so on, but afterwards I felt that perhaps they were teaching me more than I could teach them. Their so-called primitive ways of childbirth and child-rearing are like those we are rediscovering in the West, like mothers squatting to have their babies delivered in a very human way. Their traditional ways of early education were very much like those of play school which we have developed only recently. Songs and stories are sung about the history of the clan, about the creation of human beings, the creation of the world – and the children listen and sing the refrain. And I was always impressed when, for instance, a little boy of six or seven could tell me by name, say, fifty species of sweet potato. Not only could they note the differences in the leaves but also in the sweet potatoes themselves. They were educated according to nature around them.

As for my Christian faith at this time, I must say I was becoming lax. This had already started immediately after my first year as a novice, when I became so involved in philosophy and then in theology that the very zealous attitude I had had for the religious life – my praying, meditating and so on – became cold. In New Guinea the Superior of the Franciscans would tell us, 'You must always meditate,' but we said, 'When you are walking forty miles a day in the mountains or through swamps you can't meditate.' He insisted, 'You can always meditate.' However at that time I couldn't feel it and so I didn't do it. Now, because of Subud, I can meditate, as I feel an inward reality which enables me to do so.

While in New Guinea it seemed something in my Christianity was not working, though I was not conscious of it at the time. I had a neutral feeling about it. Even in a mission centre in the middle of the valley it seemed out of place to talk about spiritual things. I did preach the Good News of Christ but in a more or less revolutionary way, not at all on the same wavelength as the bishop and other priests. For instance, one of the things stipulated was building schools, because that way is the way to get people into the Church. And after the school, you build a church. But I felt it was not the time to do that, nor was I so convinced it was necessary. However, I had to do it though I couldn't personally accept the directive, which came both from the bishop and the government. We also had to introduce the Dutch language, but there was something absurd about this – these primitive boys having to learn to speak and read the language of a small and distant country. It should have been Indonesian, but at that time it was politically impossible to do that, as the official language was Dutch.

How to start a war

When in 1963 New Guinea was handed over to Indonesia we had to build Indonesian schools, as teachers were being sent out. In the Baliem Valley in one year I built twelve schools, with a house for the principal, and began preaching to those who would become the first Christians. I had myself settled on a hill in the middle of a no-man's land, and had a group of boys of fifteen or sixteen. They helped me marvellously by cutting down trees and building my house, and became the first members of my co-operative. I educated and trained them in all kinds of things, like the growing and marketing of vegetables. We built a brick factory, and later they sold bricks and money came in. I gave them lessons in Christianity.

Then, one Sunday afternoon there was a big feast and I baptised twenty-four boys. Afterwards, exhausted, I went back to the central Catholic Mission to have a free day. Next morning I came out of my bedroom to see that the whole valley in my area was covered with smoke. That was always a very bad sign, as it meant a war was going on. I went immediately to the place where they were fighting. And what did I find? What had happened was that all the boys baptised the day before had felt that the Holy Spirit had entered them and that they had to take the offensive against their enemies. They said they were being guided by the Holy Spirit and, just as the Apostles became brave after they received the Holy Spirit, they felt they were directed in the same way. So my twenty-four boys started a war. Of course I tried to put them right and they calmed down, but I felt my previous teaching must have been a failure. For me that was a very heavy day. I told the bishop that I couldn't go on doing this work, that I was not yet right for it, and that more contact work between rival groups was needed first before giving Christian teaching.

These events cooled my attitude to being a Catholic priest and giving instruction in the Catholic faith. However, I continued doing my work. I never built another church, but I liked to have a gathering of the people under a tree on Sundays in front of my house on the hill. That was their normal and natural way of gathering together. So why build a big church? If it was very rainy, we took shelter in the school.

Time to leave

I had, I believe, a good contact with the people. When in 1971 the time came to leave them and go to Jakarta, I remember thinking I wouldn't make a big drama over this. So during Mass I just said to them, 'This is the last time I shall be saying Mass here.' About 200 people attended Mass, and the top of the hill was black with them, though only the twenty-four boys had been baptised. Then I started off for the coast, but I got a letter from my successor saying, 'Please come back and say goodbye to the people properly. They have collected seven pigs for a great feast for you!' So I postponed my departure. We had a huge feast and I had to shake the hands of many, many schoolchildren, youngsters and their parents before I could get away. Hundreds of them followed me as I started my journey. First they were singing, then they became silent, and when we reached the city they started to cry. As I passed the house of the Sisters, who were looking at us pass, the Sisters were crying also.

Sometimes I think Subud works in one before one is opened. I kept having the feeling: 'I pay much attention to the people, but not enough to my own need.' At the same time I had the feeling that there was going to be a change, that something would happen.

117

In a book by Dietrich Bonhöfer I read. 'Change is grace, and fixity is sin', or something like that. It had a big effect on me. When the feelings have come so far, and you have to take a decision, everything that happens contributes towards it.

The Javanese Franciscan Superior from Jakarta came to us and said, 'It's already eight years since New Guinea has been in the hands of Indonesia, and all the Dutch priests are still working there. Why can't they come over to Indonesia, and Indonesian priests go to New Guinea? Then we would give a good example and show the Indonesian Government that we are behind their policy. Now, who would like to come back with me to Jakarta?' It was a big meeting, I remember, with many priests from everywhere in the room. I said at once, without having to think about it, 'I would like to go with you.' Everybody said to me, 'You're crazy, you can't do this when things here are going so well.' However, the Superior in New Guinea said, 'Yes you may go, and I will take over your project.'

I meet Subud

So after thirteen years in one of the most primitive parts of the world, I suddenly found myself in one of the biggest cities of Asia. On the day I arrived in the convent at Jakarta there was a newspaper in the coffee room. Inside the first page was an article about Subud and the World Congress of Subud, the opening of which had just been attended by the president of Indonesia. Forced by something inside me, I tried to find out more about it. All I knew was that it was being held in a place called Cilandak. One of the boys helping in the convent said it must be somewhere in the south. So I went south by taxi as far as the outskirts, but was still in the wrong part of the city. Next day I tried again.

After a lot of misdirections I found a place called Cilandak, but was told that there was another Cilandak, more to the west. On the third day at last I found the right Cilandak and the entrance to the Subud compound. I said that I would like to have contact with someone who could explain about Subud. I was told, 'Look, there are hundreds and hundreds of people from all over the world attending a conference. It's not a good day – all the Subud people are busy at the moment.' I said, 'I beg your pardon, but I am not going away now I have found you on the third day of searching.' Well, they arranged that I should come back and have an appointment at 10 am.

So I was met by a young Indonesian. As I talked to him I realised he had an immediate and extraordinary insight into my life, and what was missing in it, and into myself. I was really amazed. He asked, 'But why are you enquiring about Subud?' I said, almost shamefacedly, 'I've been reading the account in the newspaper.' He said, 'Well, it can be arranged. Subud can be very good for people like you.' He told me I could go to the Subud centre in Jakarta on Tuesday and Thursday evening, and after being an applicant for three months I could make my decision about joining.

The compulsory time of waiting was a very good period for me. Never in my life had I been so happy serving as a priest. The Catholic Church in Blok M became a very important church for me.

My opening in Subud was not at all dramatic, but my life afterwards became strangely different in my feelings. After nineteen years of a very low spiritual life, it was as though I became suddenly aware of what religion is. Everything became new and fresh and alive. Even when a knock came at my door at 4 am – 'Please can you take over for me? I have to say Mass at 5 o'clock at the Sisters' Convent' – I found myself saying 'Yes, thank you very much,' and doing it with pleasure, quite genuinely.

A problem with the Trinity

My faith became more living and real, but I found myself also aware more and more of what were the really essential things in religion.

Another book that became important to me at this time was Robinson's *Honest To God*, especially where his emphasis is on God being not a person but Spirit. To me it became very clear that God was One: the oneness of God became paramount and very strong – stronger than all my studies about the Trinity, and the thirteen ways of explaining it. I came to a sort of crisis. I found that I couldn't say any more, 'Glory be to the Father and to the Son and to the Holy Ghost' at the end of my Catholic prayers. I couldn't preach the sermon on Trinity Sunday any more.

So I tried to find out what was going on in me. I went to a professor of theology of the Old Testament, a very nice man and respected by the Franciscans as a holy man, and I asked him first of all to explain the Trinity. He said, 'You can say that the Trinity is a symbol. But you are right that God is One.' He said to me 'Don't make a problem over it.' But I told him, 'Well, it is a problem, because I have to explain the doctrine of the Trinity next Sunday.' He said, 'Don't make an issue over it, don't preach what I said, because it will be a shock for the community if you do so.'

The other thing that concerned me was the question of the divinity of Jesus Christ. What can you do when you can't express 'Jesus Christ is God'? I went to another colleague who was an expert in the New Testament and I said to him, 'What do you think about the divinity of Christ?' He said to me, 'And I have a question for you. Where, in the New Testament, do you find that Jesus calls himself God? He calls himself the Son of Man and the Son of God, but he never says, "I am God". So when you can't accept that he was God, never mind.' I said, 'Yes, but I am here for the people. I have to tell it to the people.' He said, 'Oh, no, man, don't do that.' So from that moment I was lame; I couldn't do anything any more.

I went to an elderly priest, who was guiding me in this crisis. He said, 'Don't preach for the time being. I give you three months off, during which you can do your social work as normally.' After the three months the feeling I couldn't go on with my work as a priest became stronger and stronger. Then I decided that the best thing to do was to go into a Trappist Abbey in Central Java for eight days, to sort myself out and to give God the opportunity to work in me in a Subud way. After six days it was clear to me what to do, but I became very afraid of the consequences. So I went to the abbot and asked, 'What would you do if you were faced with my difficulty?' He answered, 'If I were in your situation I should like to have a dispensation from Rome to leave the Order and the priesthood.'

A blessing to leave the restriction of the Church

This made a tremendous impact on me, for I came from a very Catholic family, with two sisters who were nuns and a brother who was religious. I went to another priest who was the guest-master in the abbey, and asked his advice. Without knowing what the abbot had said, he gave me exactly the same advice. That for me was enough. I left the abbey at the end of the six days.

I wrote a very open letter to my mother who had helped me to become a priest and had been a big influence on me. I took this letter to the archbishop of Jakarta and showed it to him. He said, 'Yes, I understand all you have written. But I must say that sometimes even archbishops can't say what the Will of God is in such a situation. So I can't tell you what to do. One thing I can say is that one knows a tree by its fruits. If the fruit is good, then the tree is good. And if you do good work among poor people, that is good fruit.'

So in a way he gave me a blessing and helped me to leave the restriction of the Church. But he said to me, 'Please don't stay in the middle of Jakarta, because you are well known and well liked, and if people see that you are not a priest any more this will have an impact on their faith.' I worked in a hospital for the poor of Jakarta in the western part of the city, which I could reach from the south where the Subud centre is, and in this way I could avoid the city for the next two years.

So I was not a Franciscan priest any more.

Wilbert Verheyen's story up to this point is complete in itself. The rest, perhaps, belongs in a different book. It tells how he came to live in the Cilandak compound, and grew close to Bapak. Realising he must live a normal life as a man, he married an Indonesian, Suwartini. They adopted two children, then had three of their own. He continued his social work, involving more and more Subud people, remaining throughout an extremely committed Christian. Eventually in 1983 Bapak appointed him to head Susila Dharma International, the charitable wing of Subud. Under his inspirational chairmanship it gradually developed from strength to strength. (see page 30).

Christianity, Subud and psychology

Reflecting on my Subud experience as a Christian, or my Christian experience as a Subud member, what has seemed to me essential is the profound unity in my life between my religious path as a Catholic, my Subud experience, the way I live committed in my marriage to a Muslim and also in my work as a professional psychologist in accordance with my talent. Only God, who is the source of this, can show the way.

For me everything began in the intense Catholic atmosphere of a very devout family and a personal commitment from childhood to all the religious activities of prayer, study and action in various movements. Then, in an unexpected way came my meeting and my marriage with a foreigner from a Muslim family. This marriage, very unusually, obtained a blessing as much from the very strict Muslim side as from the Catholic one, where a special dispensation from Rome was granted which enabled us to be married in a Catholic church by my own brother, a priest, who spoke appropriately of a 'sign of the times'.

But soon, a deeper unity was destined for us: at the time of our first work together as psychologists, we had a strong inner experience together which brought us to search actively afterwards for a spiritual path. Our search was to lead us several months later to being opened in Subud. The latihan, the life of Subud, is thus for us the expression of a practice, of discoveries and proofs lived together.

Allowed to take risks

What has become of my religion? For me, I must say that it has lost that formality of observance that I tried very much to respect in the past, in order to gain in depth both in spirit and in sharing.

To believe in the love of Christ has been for me the only support which has allowed me to take risks in my life, even up to the present. The first was to meet someone of another religion without fearing to lose my identity and religious values. The second has been to commit myself to Subud and to practice submission to God. The third way has been to use my talent, and through that to act in the world in the practice of our own enterprise.

With Subud and the latihan God has become a more intimate Presence, more astonishing, more demanding still. In other words, an actual felt Presence of a taste quite different from that well known from the prayer of the heart. It is really, as Bapak says, 'The Life within our Life'. And then, more and more, it is the discovery of the quality of our own inner life, and also already, from time to time, a taste of that of others; through these the discovery of our true relationship with God, the beginning of a real encounter in joy, while having to surmount obstacles to attain it. For me to live that is to approach nearer and nearer to the truth of the teaching of all religions.

Prayer is always there, but renewed. There are the same words from the Bible, particularly the Psalms, which I am rediscovering, but now they spring up from a deeper source of understanding. Like many in Subud, I believe, I allow myself to be guided in my prayers and my readings and thus I receive messages which are alive and appropriate to the moment which help me in my life and renew my wonder, my thankfulness and my adoration of God.

The bond of sharing

In my Subud life, Christ is ever-present. My opening was under the sign of the Cross and only today do I understand its symbols better: for me the vertical of the Cross represents the exclusive and privileged bond between Man and the Power of God, whereas the horizontal arm is the bond of sharing and love between all men. Christ through his perfect and unique nature has made these bonds real for us in a mysterious way. But it is to these same bonds that he invites us and constantly draws us. The latihan makes me hear this call ever more clearly, and even my work brings me closer to it.

There is profound unity in my life between my religion, Subud, my marriage and my work: sometimes, in the course of my therapeutic group-work I am surprised to find myself reciting inwardly a prayer to the Virgin Mary. Thus my work leads to prayer, and prayer suffuses my work. To work with my talent is to meet and accompany others on the human path that we must all travel and help them as best I can with what I myself have been able to understand. This task is very demanding for it asks for my own change to continue and also our development as a couple in the act of working together.

I have never understood so well as through my work the importance of certain Christian values, for example the beginnings of transcending egoism by the sharing of what one possesses with others. This comes back to Bapak's advice to be careful to share what we have with others, be it our wealth, our knowledge or anything else.

In our workshops, forgiveness takes a central place, particularly forgiveness of those who are closest and dearest to us (our parents, our marriage partners). Its growth, its expression and the benefits which flow from it are certainly one of the most marvellous things for me to experience. The discovery by modern psychology of the necessity of forgiving one's parents in order to be able to realise oneself brings back in a new form the most important teachings of the Bible, especially the New Testament, and of the Koran. What a joy for me when the participants, otherwise deeply involved in worldly things, recognise it, and come to me saying, 'If I understand well, is what you and your husband are saying what Christ said?' Or again when participants, up until now alienated from God in their lives, feel his Presence again strongly through their experience in the workshops. It is then that a deep thankfulness to God rises in our hearts.

HR

123

An Anglican's journey into Subud and the Orthodox Church

I was brought up as an Anglican Protestant, with strong Huguenot traditions, and was fairly well instructed in the Bible (with strictly literal interpretations!) and Prayer Book, but as I grew up it all seemed lifeless, as did words in church, beautiful perhaps, but without meaning or relevance. How many young people must have felt the same! But something was missing from life; I felt it must have some meaning. A chance reading of the book *An Experiment with Time* by J.W. Dunne, led me on to an eager reading of the books of PD Ouspensky and later came the opportunity to join a group studying the work of Gurdjieff. From there, in 1957, I came to Subud, and finally, some ten years ago, to the Greek Orthodox Church. That is the brief outline, and one might well ask were all those intermediate steps necessary? It is all a matter of one's eyes being opened to 'see' what is there, like the old fables of travellers who searched the world for some special treasure, and who finally returned and found it there, at home, where it had been all the time.

After some years in Subud I began to feel that the twice weekly latihan was somehow stagnating, that more of a framework was needed to help me forward; and then I began to see that this is just what the Church provides. Week by week it builds up a complete yearly cycle, not only of commemoration, but of worship and effort a cycle which one hopes, by grace, will become an upward spiral, not just a repetition.

My first vivid 'insight' came one time during a latihan when the words 'O, come, let us fall down, and kneel before the Lord our Maker' came to my mind with extraordinary impact and meaning. It was no longer simply a familiar phrase. It meant what it said, and the latihan was a means of fulfilling it. It seems such a simple thing, but the difference is hard to express in words; only someone who has experienced the same sort of thing will understand, and will know how other words take on a new meaning too.

Later on, during a period of considerable tension and physical danger, when my husband, R, was unavoidably far away, and our house in Cyprus being in a battle area with cross-fire and off-target napalm bombs being only some of the threats to our survival, I experienced an extraordinary feeling of something in me, not 'myself' taking over, and directing me as to what to do and what to say. I knew with certainty that I must make efforts to the utmost limit of my capacity to counter the threats, and at the same time that these efforts were totally inadequate by themselves, and that our only hope was in the protection of Almighty God. If He wished us to survive, we would, and if not, not. Each day seemed to bring a different kind of crisis, and as each day and each crisis passed, and we were still unharmed, I felt that only the language of the Psalms could express the surge of thanksgiving and joy that came overriding the fears.

Those same Psalms that are sung with such dreary incomprehension in many churches! Since then I believe that the necessity of making the necessary efforts and of trusting to God, apply to all our everyday situations too. During the two months approximately before R was able to get home again (normal communications being still impossible) he was able to feel through 'testing' that I was protected.

In the course of his many addresses, Bapak has several times said that the latihan can give people an understanding of their own religion; that a Christian can be a better Christian because of it, a Hindu a better Hindu, and so on. He has also urged people to pray in whatever form prayers are valid for them. Looking back at my own life (from the vantage point of my seventies) I believe that this is one of the most important aspects of the Subud way, that in fact it may be the greatest contribution from the whole Subud movement to the present century. For me, certainly, it is the most meaningful result of the latihan, and the one for which I feel the deepest gratitude, because it opened the way for me into the vast treasure house of the Christian tradition and Christian prayers.

Reading religious books, or saying the prayers, when the intellect only is involved, does not lead to real progress. Inner illumination is needed to go with it, like sunlight in a picture, colour instead of monochrome, life and warmth instead of marble statues. The latihan can and does provide this, to each one according to his capacity at the time; and with every shaft of brightness comes the humbling realisation that this is only the beginning, the first lifting of the edge of the veil; that mysteries beyond are infinite, the approach to them a pilgrimage indeed. The early Christian Fathers in their writings collected into that great work 'The Philokalia' (now available to all English speakers in a wonderful new translation) have a great deal to say about the necessity of reading the Scriptures with spiritual illumination, and of the dangers of thinking that any right understanding can come without it. It is more than sad to hear some people now speaking of the Bible as a 'dusty old book, full of quaint stories, which has no relevance to our times'. They don't know what they are missing! And as regards relevance, people have not changed much over the centuries, as even a brief reading of Roman history can show. Power struggles, corruption, oppression, injustice, pornography and more were all there, then as now. The writers of the books that form our Bible were people of real knowledge, and they wrote for all time; this is why it has survived for so long, why it is still the Book of Books.

Subud has no dogma, and does not claim to be a religion. Its purpose is the worship of Almighty God. Many parallels can be found with Christianity. To name a few, there is first of all the idea of a spiritual brotherhood, and the necessity of harmony among the members. 'Love one another', Jesus said, and this love was to be the distinguishing mark of His followers. There is the taking of a new name, as in baptism and ordination, and of importance to Subud people. There are the forty days' lenten fast and forgiveness Sunday, and the Moslem Ramadhan, both aimed at inner purification. There is the idea of perpetual latihan – St Paul said, 'Pray without ceasing'. So also was the Jesus Prayer of the Hesychasts, and the 'Practice of the Presence of God' of Brother Laurence of the seventeenth century Carmelites. The words differed, but the intention was the same. Bapak says, 'Do the latihan and your circumstances in life, and your health will improve' – and the Gospel words are, 'Seek ye first the Kingdom of God, and all else will be added unto you.' The intimate connection between the health of the body and of the soul is in both lines of thought.

After living for nearly thirty years in Cyprus, where history and human habitation have been unbroken for ten thousand years, and almost every stone has a tradition, I wondered what sort of 'atmosphere' we would find when we moved to British Columbia. Could the church, in this new country, possibly hold the same feeling of worship as that in, for instance, the small centuries-old painted churches that embellish the Cyprus landscape, and remind every village that the Aposties Paul and Barnabas once walked and preached in that country and converted the cheerful pleasure-loving pagans to a new faith? I need not have questioned. There are differences, of course, but not vital ones. The buildings are new, and the icons freshly painted – but so were all the others, once. God is here, as He is everywhere, and His peace wherever it is sought. Worship is real, and I feel blessed beyond measure to take part in it.

With humility I offer these notes as part of my thanksgiving to Almighty God.

ED

On being a Jew in Subud

It was after my tenth year in Subud when I was driving down a country road road near Monterey in California that an inner prayer began aloud: '*Shema Yisroel Adonoi Elokenu Adonoi Ehad.*' Hear O Israel, the Lord God is One. It is the central prayer of the Jewish religion, the prayer of reaffirmation, said three times a day in life and when dying before one enters eternity. It was on the lips of many of the Jews who stood in the gas chambers as they embraced God and the gases poured over them.

To be a Jew is to have God in your mouth. Whether you believe or not, God is in your mouth, either through love or fear. Soon after this inner prayer I began attending services in a small reform synagogue in Monterey. On Friday evenings the candles were lit and the sabbath prayers were said. The Rabbi was young, bright, and I enjoyed talking with him. The religious content was minimal for me but it was enough to be there for I have always enjoyed the sense of belonging which is one of the things that had attracted me to Subud.

A few months later I found myself in San Diego. After living with a Subud brother for the first few months after my arrival, I took an apartment alone. I had continued to attend reform services on Friday night. The temple was much larger and I felt more anonymous. I began to experience that I should remain close to home on Saturdays and then later that I should not travel on Friday nights.

I became more orthodox
My maternal grandmother has been orthodox while I was growing up so I had absorbed some of the traditions and observances of the law. I had not thought about it since I was a very young boy. On Friday nights I would light the candles, say prayers and sit down to eat the large meal I had prepared. I stopped using mechanized

convenience, including the phone from sundown on Friday to sundown on Saturday. At first it felt odd, but as time passed, I realized what a treat it was not to have the outside world intrude for one day in an effort to create perfect peace. All the calls from the outside world were not as important as I once had thought they were. The work world, the complicated social world, could not trespass on my serenity. Rest was guaranteed. My walks on sabbath afternoons were filled with magic. Breezes sang. Beauty was inscribed and enshrined by God's hand on everything if only to delight us. I was witness to eternal creation. It was as if I were walking around in latihan but with eyes opened. The prayer of 'Shema Yisroel' had been realised inside of me. There is One God who created the universe and everything is a part of that one God. Yet with all of this peace and beauty, I still felt a longing to share this experience.

I find the Hassidim

Years before I had met a group of Hassidim in Massachusets. They had invited me to their house for the Sabbath and I had spent many enjoyable hours with them. Now four years later I found myself thumbing through the phone book looking for their synagogue in San Diego. 'Of course,' the voice on the other end of the line said, 'spend the sabbath with us.' I began spending every weekend with them. Eventually I moved closer to the university where their community was established, for they were Lubavicher Hassidim, active in recruiting Jews to the traditional ways of Judaism. I found them to be loving, helpful, intelligent, honest, mystical, highly structured, hospitable and patient. The community contained a few married couples with children, many college students and two Hassidic Rabbis. On Friday evening we would all eat the sabbath meal together on two long tables. On Saturday afternoons, after two-hour services, single people would be invited to the homes of the married couples for the traditional afternoon meal. No one had to be alone unless they wished to. When we sang and danced together on Friday nights and on certain holidays, I could feel the latihan strongly. An old saying, 'God respects us when we work and loves us when we dance,' sounded in my head.

I found a part-time job at the university which allowed me time to read and to study the culture and the reasons behind the religious rituals and prayers. I realised that religion was a ritualised way of keeping God's name in the world. The presence of God and all the goodness associated with that name would not be forgotten. Gradually I became more orthodox, wearing the skull cap, keeping all the Kosher laws, establishing perfect rest on the sabbath and other holidays, everything to the letter of the law. I felt reborn, renewed, invigorated and spiritually cleansed.

Was I mixing?

During these two years I continued to do my latihan two or three times a week, with the group and by myself. In part, I felt divided between my two communities. I'd go to latihan with my head covered. When the Subud group had Friday night or Saturday activities I had to bow out gracefully. There was a larger question in my mind: was I mixing? I tested with the helpers and found that my religion would make me stronger. The testing helped verify an inner certainty I had been experiencing.

Two years of learning combined with the latihan was powerful. I decided that I would like to study formally, full-time at a *yeshiva*. The word *yeshiva* has its roots in the verb 'to sit'. That is, sitting, from sun up well into the late hours of the night, studying the Five Books of Moses, the laws and commentaries on the laws, reading, arguing, discussing. Serious students stay for five years or more. My learning was infinitesimal compared to the amount of literature that exists. Imagine someone with the mind of a Freud or an Einstein, dedicating his life from earliest years to learning and writing. Multiply that by thousands of years of great scholars. My learning compared to that was like a drop of rain in the midst of a downpour. Many times I would lean back in my chair and reflect that this could have been me in a similar chair with the same colleagues anywhere during the past two thousand years of history.

Is the latihan 'kosher'?

Many times statements I had heard from Bapak or I had read in his talks would be similar to what I was studying. Was it because the inner content of Judaism and Islam are similar and flowed from the same roots? Was it because Bapak's experiences led him to the same understanding as that of the many great men who had written the established teachings of how the universe functioned? I would say to myself, 'Yes, I remember Bapak saying that about the seven levels of creation and what they stood for.'

129

The dormitory life at the yeshiva didn't suit my restless personality. The overabundance of rituals caused me to feel overly confined. My mind said, 'Yes, this is where you belong.' My heart said, 'too mechanized, to ritualistic, not meant for your free spirt'. A new question arose: 'Is the latihan *kosher*?' Was it a valid experience for an orthodox Jew? I decided to gamble and ask the head Rabbis at the Yeshiva to give me their opinion. I explained Subud to them to the best of my ability. I spoke about Bapak and of my experiences in the latihan. A few days later I was told there was nothing in Subud that they would consider idol worship (the big no-no). If I wanted to continue doing the latihan it would be my own personal choice, but as far as they were concerned it was not against Jewish law.

It has been six years since that experience. Gradually I have become less ritualistic in my observances. I still pray the traditional prayers in the morning. I still keep the sabbath and do not work but rest, but I am more flexible and less traditional than I was before. I carry out my observances with love because they comes more from a place of love than requirement.

I know that many orthodox Jews would strongly disagree with what I have said. 'We accept and then we understand,' is the saying. I know for them the observance of all rituals can be a beautiful experience.

What do I conclude about being a Jew in Subud? That the latihan is a great gift for all members of all religions. That it led me to learn more about Judaism. With that understanding came a great thirst and love of knowledge which I began to fulfil. The latihan reaffirms my faith and has given me the 'experience' of the reality of God. I thank God for all I've been given and Bapak for sharing the latihan with me, for it has helped me continually to grow. And I thank you for having the patience to read to the end of this.

LL

A Benedictine monk testifies to the reality of the latihan

Père Albert Bescond, a Benedictine monk at the Abbey of St. Wandrille in Normandy, was the best-known religious person who has joined Subud. He died in 1986. He made many contributions to Subud periodicals which, with his private letters to members, will be the basis of a study which the present editor is preparing.

The following piece written in January 1962 was entitled 'A Simple Testimony' and has been slightly shortened.

For more than a year I have been asked to testify. Many have written to me, spoken to me, or sent messages to me to say that it is not easy to reconcile Subud and Christianity. The questions put to me can be reduced to two. I shall try to answer them by expressing something of what, over a period of three years, I have received from the latihan.

I hope that these few words may bring a little light and peace of mind to those Catholics who have need of them. Certainly I would not wish to impose my own experience as a line of conduct to be followed by others, and still less would I wish to dogmatise and state the 'attitude of the Church'. In fact I am not authorised to do that, nor is there anything spectacular about my Subud experience. Undoubtedly, as soon as I received the contact I was cured of vertigo, and I found myself able to swim. But after all, as a monk one might hope for more than that.

I must add, to be fair, that the practice of the latihan has built up in me a very solid stability, a deep rooting in my vocation as a monk. In particular, the reality of the Mystical Body and of the transfer of merits – which can alone justify withdrawal into the monastic life – have become for me a matter of direct experience. They are like a climate in which one lives, like the air one breathes. I do not insist upon this point: those who know will understand me; those who do not know have no need to understand, for what I have to say is something different.

But lest more importance than it deserves be ascribed to my message, I want to say first of all that testing does not give me anything. I find it marvellous that people should receive answers by way of gestures, visions and voices. Nothing of that kind happens to me. What I experience is no more than a more or less strong conviction which has nothing to do with thinking. Sometimes it is simple animal instinct, more rarely an image which could equally well be the fruit of my own imagination. That is all. Nevertheless, one of these instinctive impulses has led me to write today. I believe that in giving way to it I am doing what is right. May I be forgiven if I am mistaken.

Bapak's explanations and Christian faith

Some Catholics are perturbed because certain explanations given by Bapak about Christ, about prayer and about sin and so on, do not agree with what is taught in the Church. I also was for a moment worried about such things at the beginning, but it seems to me that I have now understood and I believe that there is no problem. The truth is that Bapak does not speak in the way priests do, that is, as a theologian. He does not seek to state a dogma, a revealed truth communicated to him by God in order to inaugurate a new religion. He places himself upon a different plane, that of spiritual experience itself. We have perhaps too much forgotten that every one of the truths of our creed has two aspects, one dogmatic and one experiential. Priests have perhaps insisted too much on the dogmatic aspect to the point of forgetting or allowing to be forgotten, the side that concerns experience, and so for many people spiritual life is divided in two: on one side there is a more or less theoretical and abstract belief and on the other side an experience of life, more or less joyful or anguished. Subud heals this division. But Bapak is very careful not to encroach upon the territory of the priest. What he shows us is the side of experience.

Let us take an example: the priest who speaks of sin will say to you. 'This is an offence against God, a failure in love towards God. In order to repair this you should receive the Sacrament of Penance, which will give Grace back to you and will re-establish you in your baptismal dignity as a son of God.'

On the same subject Bapak expresses himself quite differently: 'Sin is an impurity of your inner state (*rasa diri*). In order to put it right, you receive the latihan which will give you a contact with the Great Force of Life, and will re-establish you in your dignity as a complete man (*sempurna*).'

In this there is no opposition. The two points of view complete one another. The first presents things from the side of God, it is the dogmatic aspect of sin. The other presents things from the point of view of man, it is the experienced aspect of sin. The total truth includes the combination of these two aspects, both of which are true. As a proof of that I can say this to you: try the experience of the Sacrament of Penance, and try the experience of the latihan, and you will understand for yourself.

These interventions of Bapak in the domain of experience concerning the truths of our faith, far from being regrettable are on the contrary salutary. I appeal again to the experience of Catholics. How many times have you heard it said (and perhaps have said yourselves): 'It is discouraging, I am inclined to anger, to sensuality and so on. I frequently come to receive the Sacrament of Penance, but this does not cure me. What is the use of the Sacrament?'

To those of you who are in Subud I can reply very easily thanks to the explanations given by Bapak: 'Your experience is right, the Sacrament does not cure you. Do not expect from the Sacrament that for which it is not intended. The Sacrament is a rite which re-establishes your dignity as the child of God. It repairs your failure in love towards God, but it is not given to us for the reconstitution of our human integrity, to purify our inner state (at any rate directly). It operates in regions of your being which are inaccessible to your consciousness.

It is the latihan that can give you the healing which can be observed, but on the other hand *the latihan cannot in the ordinary course of things be the instrument of Grace* in the Catholic meaning of the term, because as Bapak himself has said, Subud is a technique, whereas Grace is a free gift of God which is not tied to any technique.

The gift of the latihan and the gift of grace

I have just italicised the words 'in the ordinary course of things, the latihan is not an instrument of Grace'. This is a delicate problem but we have to face it (in order to be complete, it would be necessary to explain also the words 'at any rate directly', which I put in parenthesis in the last but one paragraph, but I must keep within limits).

This question in reality is not so theoretical as it seems. Many of us are able to testify that it is part of our deepest experience in Subud, and peace in our own progress and in our relations with our non-Christian brothers depends in part at least upon its solution. Let me say at once that the solution is not something that we have to find. It already exists, and it is enough to become conscious of it. It is this becoming conscious that I want to help those who need it to reach.

There is as a matter of fact a question which interferes with the good development of the latihan among certain people: 'Why,' they say, 'is the contact with the Great Force of Life not given us in the Name of Jesus Christ, since all Grace comes to us through Him?'

In order to reply to this question, it is necessary to have experience both of the latihan and also of the Sacraments. Those who have this double experience are able to know that the Life given by the Sacraments is the very Life of God the Trinity, and that this Life is in itself beyond all human experience. Even the mystics are quite unable to perceive this Life, excepting perhaps in a negative way, and if something is experienced it is not this Life in itself, but only its effects. God is too far above us to be apprehended by any means whatever, but Faith assures us that He is present in the Sacraments and in the justified soul. Here we are in the realm of the Redemption, and this gift is the work of the Redeemer, Jesus Christ, God and man. On the other hand, the Great Life Force received in the latihan is something which we experience. It is therefore not the Life of God Himself, it is a life which animates the whole creation and which comes from God, as does everything that exists in the universe. It is a gift of God, but a gift different from Grace, one which involves God not as Redeemer but as Creator. It seems to me that Bapak always speaks of God as the Creator.

Ways of giving

There are in truth many ways of giving: a man can give his money, or simply a kind word, but he can also give his daughter in marriage, and that is more serious, because it is his blood and his life which he is giving. In the same way God can give to humanity His own life in order to lead us to redemption by Christ the Saviour (this is the experience which we have in the Sacraments). But He can also give to humanity, simply, the Riches of His creation, in order to bring mankind to Fullness in the order of his true nature (and this is the experience that we have in the latihan). There Christ appears in the role of the perfected man (as Bapak himself said at the World Congress in London).

In other words, the contact is not given in the Name of Jesus Christ, because this contact is a gift of God the Creator. God is acting as the Lord of Riches. The Sacraments are given in the Name of Christ because they are a gift of God the Redeemer. Here God acts as the Father who gives His Life.

I add a few important insights that have been given to me in the latihan. Apart from a few exceptions I have not had visions nor have I heard voices. What happens to me takes the form rather of an illumination in the depth of the soul; that is all that I have to communicate. I do not know if it is valid; you who read must judge.

I wish to say in the hope of coming to a better mutual comprehension, that it can happen and that it does in fact happen, that the latihan can be the occasion of a Grace, in the sense that the Catholic Church uses this word. For Grace is given to non-Christians just as much as to Christians.

Let us remain with the facts of our experience. We all know that it is not by our own powers that we are able to stop in ourselves the working of our passions, our desires and our thoughts. The Yogi tries to do it by his ascetic practice, but we do not even try to do this. All our attention – Bapak insists on this point – is directed to one objective only, submission to God. We know very well that objectively our submission is far from being perfect; nevertheless we try to live it, or more exactly to receive it, with sincerity, patience and perseverance. This is the fundamental religious attitude from the Shema of Israel and the Hypotagi of our Fathers, to the Bhakti of India (that *bhakti* that Bapak puts before us as the aim of the latihan and which is not exactly 'worship' but rather 'devoted service' as I have seen it admirably translated in Subud literature) without forgetting certainly the significance of the Moslem word (Qur'an Surat 3.v.64). Now it is the common doctrine that such a moral discipline as this cannot be realised concretely without a supernatural help from God (this is what is called 'actual Grace').

Let me be well understood: I do not affirm that all those who do the latihan automatically receive a Grace, just as we may also suppose that certain people can have spectacular manifestations without having real submission to God. But once this reserve has been made (and it is necessary to insist on it if it were a question of describing the Subud phenomena, but this is not my aim here), we should recognise that whoever truly makes the act of submission to God does receive Grace in order to be able to do it, and he could not make this act of submission without Grace. The prolonged experience of the latihan teaches us that these acts of submission end by becoming a habit, and the soul after a time, which may be short or long, enters into a continuous state of inward submission (to Divine inspiration) and outward submission (to the Commandments of God). This no doubt comes from the fact that the inner self is purified and all the inner forces are made quite and harmonious. This is the true fruit of the latihan.

Whether Christian or not

Now this constant submission is directed, not to some natural force, but to God Himself, to the living God, to the God of Abraham, which is, whether one knows it or not, the God of Jesus Christ. Again it must be recognised that such an attitude is not possible without Grace, and all those who live habitually in this submission to the living God, we know that they are justified, that they are children of God, that their purified being is the temple of the Holy Spirit – whether they are Christian or not. We should therefore have a great respect for one another.

You may say to me 'In this case what need is there of practising the Sacraments?' I will reply very simply: there are those who know and those who do not know. God comes to whom He will. Whoever knows what a Sacrament is and despises it in the name of the latihan, does something which is contrary to submission, and in consequence he destroys in himself all that submission could have brought him. To receive a Sacrament is to make a further step in submission and to dispose oneself to receive a greater grace. I call on the experience of my very dear friends who have followed Subud without the Sacraments, and now follow it with the Sacraments. These things are not to be explained. They have to be lived. But for those who do not know what a Sacrament is, and who cannot know it perhaps because we are the screen that shuts out the light, the Lord will not reject their submission, only He fills them with His gifts without revealing the wholeness of what He has given them. They may believe that they have to thank the latihan alone for a gift which infinitely surpasses the latihan and which can only come from the immeasurable riches of the Heart of Christ on the Cross. This is for us the true significance of the Cross, but we cannot complain of their ignorance, and I beg that they should not see anything offensive in these words. I do not think myself better than others because of what I know.

There is in this truth a mystery of predestination. In a latihan the question came to me, 'Why should so and so and so and so who are such pure souls, not ask to receive the sign of Christ and enter into the way of the Cross?' and a reply was given to me in the form of a feeling of humility that I had not previously suspected. Then I was able to understand what is truly that which we call the 'baptism of desire', which is psychologically very different from the desire for baptism. One day they will understand. It will be the great revelation, the great Epiphany which will come one day for those who have followed Christ without knowing it. Our faith tells us that the Church in triumph in the Heavens is composed not only of Christians who went right through with their Christianity, but also with those Jews, Moslems, Hindus, Buddhists and all other men of good will who have gone beyond the limits of their respective religions.

Let us remember also that our Christianity will not be of any value to us for the life beyond if we do not allow ourselves to be carried by the Spirit beyond the human limitations of our own Christianity.

Epiphany 1962
F. Albert Bescond

For a time Père Bescond worked with a small team of French members on a translation of Bapak's main work, Susila Budhi Dharma. *On one occasion the present editor passed on to him a letter from a French Catholic friend, PG, in which he wrote, 'Anything which can unite mankind ought to be carefully investigated, but it appears to me from the brochure you sent me that Subud is more centred on the individual search for personal development than on the glory of God, the former not excluding the latter, of course, but being subordinated to it.'*

Père Bescond replied:

To Monsieur G one could answer that God has no greater glory than the perfection of his creatures: everything which in this world contributes to this perfecting by this very fact contributes to the glory of the Creator, who is at once both the author of man who benefits from the latihan, and of the latihan which perfects man. I have always dreamt of having the time to evaluate the perspectives of the book *Susila Budhi Dharma*, where Bapak expresses himself best. This book is truly 'theocentric', for throughout it is always a matter of obtaining the means to receive help from God, of giving ourselves entirely to God. One can say that in this book God is alpha and omega, the beginning and the end, for everything comes from Him and returns to Him. In marriage man is presented as a 'channel' for the divine force which he receives from God and which he propagates in humanity. Bapak also has a sacred conception of culture, because for him every development of man is an effort to accept His will and the construction of the world and of society as the design of God in action. I even ask myself if Christians in the twentieth century are not in danger of forgetting God's place in their activities and in the goals of their action.

Some theological questions raised by the latihan

The author is Assistant Professor of Religious Studies at Seton Hall University, New Jersey USA.

The question of how to describe the relation of Subud and religion is a difficult one. It was not Bapak's way to provide theological formulations about the nature of the latihan because he wanted members to come to the experience of the latihan with as few preconceived notions about it as possible. And it is clear that one does not need theological formulations to experience the latihan. There are countless examples of people who experienced their opening in a 'spontaneous' fashion; people who experienced their opening despite infirmity or other limitations to discursive thought; people who experienced their opening in the presence of helpers with whom there was no linguistic or cultural commonality; people who experienced their opening without even an affirmation of belief in 'God'; we have stories of Subud coming to people who had no religious faith and were merely asked if they were willing to surrender to the 'Truth'. To illustrate this: a well-known Indonesian Communist came to argue with Bapak that Subud must be a hoax because it implied the existence of God, which had been disproved by modern science. Bapak asked him: 'Do you want to know the Truth, whatever it may be?' The Communist agreed then and there, while scoffing at the idea he might be taken in. At his first latihan he was profoundly moved and came back again and again. After some months he admitted receiving such decisive evidence of the spiritual world of God and the soul that he abandoned atheistic materialism and became a devoted member of Subud. (Bennett, *Christian Mysticism and Subud*, p6.)

The writer's three point approach

Speaking of different religious traditions with their own truth claims might suggest that I am outside these circles of concern. In fact, by profession and by religious faith I fall into at least three circles: I am in Subud and have been doing the latihan for sixteen years. I am a practising Christian, and I am an 'academic', having concentrated on Christian theology and scripture during my undergraduate years, and on Islamic theology during my doctoral work.

As a Subud member with helper reponsibilities I must ever learn to speak with members and non-members about the latihan in ways that are sensitive, accurate and experience-based.

As a Christian I have to find ways of 'reconciling' not just Subud with my religion but all other claims of authentic religious experience outside the Christian one. This desire to – or problem of – reconciling the ontological claims of the plurality of religions is a subject being pursued today by many serious theologians of all the major religions. In a sense, though, it is the very sharing of the latihan with people of different tongues, cultures and creeds that forces us in Subud to think about the nature of what it is that is being shared.

As an academic and teacher of world religions, I have come to appreciate the rich and varied emphases that the traditions hold dear and by which they define themselves. I am also quite aware that theological positions which have come to be seen as orthodox are themselves dependent on time and historical development and subject to variation and change and interpretation. I also know that, although it is said by Subud members that Subud has no theology, there are no statements about the spiritual life or practice – or anything for that matter – that are not without presuppositions about the nature of reality and the ultimate source of being. I doubt that any Subud member would have been opened had not they 'had faith' that the God to whose will they were about to surrender was a 'good' God and not an evil, capricious one – one of the many 'theological' presuppositions of 'surrender' in latihan.

Our responsibility with words as well as in actions

I am also aware that, as Subud becomes known in the world, it will be studied by people outside Subud and, if Subud does not find ways of critically examining and expressing its own world view and theological perspective, others outside of Subud will. With Bapak gone, we must recognise the grave responsibilities we share in introducing Subud to others – yes, with our actions, but also with our words. We who have experienced the latihan know the infinite variety of effects of the latihan, but the latihan is not just anything.

Part of my Subud experience was finding my vocation in world religion studies. And I suspect that part of my vocation will be to address the nature of Subud within the context of the religious and academic worlds. I am not sure at all that what is called for is a 'reconciling' of religion, for example, my Christian faith or someone else's Islamic faith, with Subud. I think that most of the people who have contributed to this book are not talking about theological reconciliation. In other words reconciling in the sense of ideological agreement. They are talking about the personal experiences in both their Subud and their 'religious' worlds that engendered a feeling of harmony between the two.

Being in the right place

In these 'Evidences' Subud members speak of how elements of Judaism, Christianity and Islam sometimes flow together for them. I do not think, however, that this means there must be an emphasis on common ground, or that 'mutuality' is the way to describe, from a Subud perspective, the relation of religious traditions. For to focus on 'mutuality' might offend some; to focus on the particularity and exclusivity of religions might offend others. I do, however, agree with the main conclusion of this book that the emphasis should be – rather, is – on us 'being in our right place'. This, I believe, is a more adequate means of describing the personal orientation and growth process which is the consequence of following the latihan. We are taken on a complete and sometimes subtle journey, or movement of our soul, to find a place where it can be at home in the world of cultural forms in accordance with its (our 'inner') nature, predispositions and realisations.

What this has meant for me, regarding my feelings towards Christianity and Christ is that the latihan has opened up, and continues to open up, new dimensions of understanding of 'content-feeling', about Scripture, liturgy, and even the 'world of the mind', ie theology. But even my involvement with Christianity has had its changes, its movements. I have noticed that my early latihan days seemed to engender feelings of peace and insight at Mass – and an ability to overlook the human problems that any institution embodies. My latihan of late has brought me to really question particular attitudes and institutional problems within the Church. And so my instinct is that I am now being guided, prompted, to become more vocal in expressing these concerns.

What I have found interesting, and what convinces me that there is really an element of 'one's true nature' at stake – a nature that we each must experience for ourselves – is that despite differences or concerns I have felt towards my religion, I truly feel that I am at the core a Christian. My feelings at a quiet Eucharist are deeper than I can express. I have great affection and admiration for a certain all-encompassing beauty I find in many forms of Christian piety and thought. I am inspired by contemplating the lives of the saints.

So how can I feel thus and devote my professional life to the study of other religions, especially Islam? Does this relate to the question of Subud and religion?

Different truth claims transcended

Whenever I speak to applicants about Subud's attitude toward religion (that people may pursue their own religion; that the 'content' of all religions is one, and so on) I always begin by admitting that I don't know how this can 'work out' given the natural exclusivity of religious claims. I mean, after all, religions usually – perhaps always – emerge in response, reaction, or rejection of preceding or presiding religions. That is reality in human existence. Does Subud diminish these claims in asserting a kind of transcendence of those claims? Perhaps this is the crux and what even separates people in Subud on the issue of religion. (By the latter, I mean that it can be offensive to people who do participate in traditional forms of religion when particular truth claims are rejected in favour of universal assimilatist claims, claims that say one religion 'includes' or embraces another, or that new religious movements transcend the old ones.)

I believe that in fact, Subud's claim is that somehow our latihan transcends cultural/religious differences without obliterating or even diminishing them. *Somehow* is a key word because we do not know the metaphysical scheme by which it works, yet many of us have experienced the truth of this claim. *Somehow* I, as a believing Christian, can do latihan with a Buddhist or Muslim or Jew, and feel the integrity of their truth claims. I know that *somehow* there must be a point of unity to these truth claims, not just because there must be an ontological source of both unity and diversity (what my religion professors would say), but because I have sensed the truth of that unity. This sense of unity cannot be proven. It is a unity that is intuited and which seems to defy what linguists, philosophers and social scientists tell us: that there can be no ontological, psychological, or sociological points of unity outside of chance historical connections.

No fundamentalists in Subud

I have of late become very suspicious of theories – even from Subud members – which attempt to capsualise the situation. *Mystery, tentativeness, process* must be part of the picture as to why we insist that no one is required to leave their religion, and why in fact involvement in religion can be of benefit (if that involvement emphasises surrender and if it provides a learning experience for the member as to the complex interrelation, distinction and needs of the heart, mind and soul).

I think it is fair to tell people that, although we have members from virtually all religions in Subud, the vast majority seem to have a receptivity toward new understandings and empathy vis-a-vis their own tradition and other traditions. If we don't seem to have religious fundamentalists [except in the sense of SA, page 105, – Ed.] this is clearly because fundamentalism demands a static concept of religious truth and experience. Some of us could even be called religious 'conservatives', if by this term we mean that we participate in and appreciate the traditions that have been handed down to us which still hold meaning for us and whose meaning we see grounded in God's ultimacy and divine grace.

This does not mean that we don't observe change, historical development, institutional and human needs at work in those cultural forms and traditions. This I see as very compatible with what Bapak has said about religion. Fundamentalism, on the other hand, holds a usually romanticised (usually inaccurate) view of the formation of religion and its belief and practices which is clung to, I suppose out of fear, as a possession. Perhaps the crux is that the person's attitude toward religion in general will make the difference in their response to the idea that Subud holds in balance both universal and exclusive religious claims. Religion as 'process' versus religion as 'possession' is one way of thinking about it.

I realise that while my latihan experience may be beyond words my ordinary life and its conversation with the rest of the world demand my trying to make at least an adequate expression of the paradoxically tentative yet not arbitrary nature of the latihan and its workings in my life. I have come to feel that it is precisely because God's nature is mysterious, infinite and utterly transcendent that our own expressions about God and even about our own experiences will have a tentative quality to them. I prefer the idea of a holy tentativeness over the idea of a locked-in orthodoxy on the one hand or pure relativism on the other.

GW

Epilogue

Bapak Muhammad Subuh, the founder of Subud, died in June 1987, forty years after Subud was named and registered in Indonesia. Bapak was the bringer of the latihan and our spiritual guide and no one could, or tried to, succeed him. Subud has, therefore, been going through the testing period that follows the death of the founder of any spiritual movement.

Only a small body of members exists as yet, clustered or dotted thinly across the world in some seventy countries. At first we found ourselves looking to and at each other at our meetings with a mixture of wonder, hope and doubt. Could it really be that the continuation of this gift of unexpected grace which had come into the world through the exemplary, surrendered life of a Javanese Muslim depended on us, on our faithfulness and effectiveness? Bapak had told us, 'You yourselves will replace Bapak'. This is a daunting challenge that only makes it clearer that we of ourselves alone can achieve nothing, that we can only pass on this spiritual contact if it is really working and manifesting in our own lives.

Ibu Rahayu, Bapak's daughter, is held in the highest respect. When consulted she gives a continual example of humility, spiritual wisdom and common sense. She encourages us not to imitate Javanese religious and cultural traditions just because Bapak followed them.

Some grandiose illusions have been shattered. In the area of Subud I know best we are learning, when things do not work out, to pick up the pieces without rancour. Some of us are more likely than others to receive signs and revelations and to live by them, but we all, I think, come to see that we develop by accepting that the Subud way is a process, often painful, of self-knowledge and change. 'Sacrifice,' Bapak has said, in a typically dynamic phrase, 'is action for change'. We are helped by the latihan and by sharing with each other to shed our fears and angers, our personal imaginings, our self-love, and to clean the slate of the results of our own and our forbears' faulty living. At the same time, we can hope to discover and develop our own creative talents and become more free to live according to our own natures.

As regards the main theme of this book, Subud, in Bapak's words, 'has come into the world to bring harmony into all religions so that, in their totality, they represent one human family, one aim and one God'. This will happen, not through any new teachings, for all the necessary teaching has already been given. Rather, the experience of the living, inner reality of the worship of the one God could gradually bring to an end all religious division and conflict.

Bapak, however, was no Utopian visionary but a realist about human limitations. He would say, for instance, 'If fifty per cent is achieved, that is already good!' and 'Do as much as is possible.' Man will remain man; conflicts, even wars, will go on.

Subud makes no propaganda, no claims. The only proof is in the being and the visible fruits of those who practise the latihan. Will Subud soon expand? We can only work and wait in faith. Many of us think we are not ready yet, not together and strong enough to take on large numbers. It could be otherwise, and that we need this challenge. But I do believe, deep inside, that to which this book tries to bear witness – too heavily perhaps, with too many words – the possibility of a future world towards which the thinking and feeling, the work, the longing and prayers of innumerable people, consciously or unconsciously, are converging.

If this is where Subud points, where does it come from? When Bapak was first in England, someone remarked on the rapidity with which a foreign movement was being assimilated. Bapak replied:

> Subud is not foreign. It belongs to no country, just as it belongs to no race or creed. It did not 'originate' in the East, it did not 'come' to the West. It comes from the Spirit of God, which is nowhere a stranger. So when we arrived in England we did not feel ourselves as foreigners, nor did you feel that we were strangers from a strange land. From the beginning we could be like brothers, because there is one and only One Spirit that works in us all. That is the true meaning of Subud.

> (J.G. Bennet, *Concerning Subud*, p. 69)

Glossary

Certain Sanskrit, Indonesian and English words are very important in Subud because of the use that Bapak made of them. Since he defined them in a fresh way again and again, there are no standard definitions or translations. The following short glossary, however, may be helpful.

Subud   (for origin of word see page 11) a symbol for the possibility of man to follow the right way of living. A world-wide spiritual association of those who worship the One God Almighty, submitting themselves to him through the *latihan kejiwaan*. All of humanity under the Grace of God. (No connection with the name of the founder.) Subud contains a trinity of three Sanskrit words: *Susila, Budhi, Dharma*.

Susila   the qualities which give rise to a character, conduct and actions which are truly human and in accordance with the will of God.

Budhi   the highest power that exists in man, separate from heart and mind. The divine spark or essence in every creature. A pure, inner feeling that can easily receive what is needed and will be needed. The content of all true understanding.

Dharma   (not as in Indian philosophy) the possibility for every creature, including man, to submit to the will of God, with patience, trust and sincerity; the reality of inner feeling that enables someone to do this.

latihan   Indonesian for 'training' or 'exercise'.

jiwa   the inner content of the entire self. Sometimes translated as 'soul'.

kejiwaan   relating to the *jiwa*, often translated as 'spiritual'.

the nafsu   the passions; the life forces that animate feeling and thinking.

shariat   Islamic prayers and observances conducted outwardly.

tarekat   worship with understanding of the inner significance of worship.

hakekat   worship penetrating to the reality of truth; inner awareness of the power of God, of the Great Life.

Bapak   Father – the usual address in Indonesia to an older and respected man.

helpers   originally chosen by Bapak to be his own helpers in explaining, spreading and maintaining the purity of the *latihan kejiwaan*; now serving Subud in this way.

opening   the first contact with the latihan, passed on in the presence of helpers.

testing   see page 22.

Cilandak   Bapak's home until 1986 and the Subud centre for Indonesia.

References

Apologies for incomplete or missing references

1. Reference not found
2. London, 17 August 1959 (tape ref: 59 LON 2)

Part 1 – Introduction to Subud

1. Psalm 22, verse 30
2. Subud International Archives, ref Hist disc 1, symbol 2
3. Coombe Springs, England, 19 August 1959 (59 CSP 9)
4. *Antidote*, p. 6 (see bibliography)
5. Jakarta, 29 June 1984 (84 JKT 4)
6. Melbourne, 7 May 1982 (82 MEB 4)
7. Cilandak, Indonesia, 28 June 1984 (84 CDK 8)
8. Wendhausen, Germany, May 2nd 1981
9. Wolfsburg, Germany, 15 June 1972 (72 WOB 1)
10. Woodstock, USA, 12 September 1977 (77 WOS 1)
11. Condensed from a number of quotes:
    Wolfsburg, 15 June 1972 (72 WOB 1)
    Colombo, Sri Lanka, March 1981
    Anugraha, England, 15 August 1983
    Jakarta, 7 July 1984 (84 CDK 13)
12. Cilandak, Indonesia, 13 December 1969 (69 TJK 14)
13. Brisbane, 24 January 1978 (78 BNE 3)
14. Coombe Springs, England, 24 August 1959 (59 CSP 12)
15. Anugraha, England, 10 August 1983
16. Vancouver, 17 July 1981 (81 VVR 4)
17. Hamburg, 20 September 1983 (83 HAM 3)
18. Melbourne, 30 April 1982 (82 MEB 1)
19. Details of this section from *Remembrances of Bapak's Last Days* (see bibliography)
20. Jakarta, 24 June 1985

Part 2 – Bapak Speaks

1. *Susila Budhi Dharma* (see bibliography)
2. San Francisco, 26 March 1958 (58 SFO 1)
3. Chicago, June 1959

4. Coombe Springs, England, 10 August 1959 (59 CSP 2)
5. Vienna, 8 December 1959 (59 VIE 1)
6. Singapore, April 1960
7. New York City, 16 July 1963 (63 BCL 7)
8. New York City, 9 July 1963 (63 BCL 2)
9. Planegg, Germany, 6 August 1964 (64 PLG 2)
10. Brisbane, reference not found
11. Jakarta, June 29 1984
12. From a letter, dated 1969
13. Letter in *Pewarta* VII, vol. 4, pp. 25–7, 1970
14. Cilandak, Indonesia, 27 October 1972 (72 TJK 7)
15. Wolfsburg, Germany, June 1975
16. Cilandak, Indonesia, January 1981
17. London, 10 April 1981
18. Hamburg, 17 September 1983 (83 HAM 1)
19. Cilandak, Indonesia, 9 August 1984 (84 CDK 17)
20. Cilandak, Indonesia, 11 June 1986
21. Cilandak, Indonesia, 11 November 1986 (86 CDK 11)
22. Skymont, Virginia, USA, August 1970
23. October/November 1990, in *Subud Voice*, January 1991

Select Bibliography

Bancroft, Anne; Twentieth Century Mystics and Sages (Heinemann 1976 and Penguin 1990)

Bennett, John; Concerning Subud (Hodder and Stoughton 1958)

Bennett, John; Subud and Christian Mysticism (Coombe Springs Press 1961)

Keele, Luqman; Journey Beyond the Stars (Starlight Press Sydney 1989)

Lyle, Robert; Subud (Humanus 1983)

Lyle, Robert; A Way Through the World (Altamira 1985)

Pope, Salamah; Antidote (SPI 1989)

Rieu, Dominic; A Life Within a Life (Humanus 1983)

Rieu, Dominic; And Other Secret Things (Redcliffe 1985)

Rofé, Husein; The Path of Subud (Ryder 1959)

Smart, Harris; Nineteen Steps (Starlight Press, Sydney 1989)

Subud Publications International (SPI) Remembrances of Bapak's Last Days (1987)

Sullivan, Matthew Barry; Groundwork for Caring (Humanus 1983), Report and Survey of Susila Dharma International Association (ed) 1991

Sumohadiwidjojo, Muhammad Subuh; Susila Budhi Dharma (SPI 1959, 1972 and 1991)

van Hien, Edward; What is Subud? (Ryder 1963)

Vittachi, Tarzie Varindra; A Reporter's Assignment in Subud (SPI 1971)

Vittachi, Tarzie Varindra; Bouquets for Bapak: a Memoir of Subud (SPI 1989)

von Bissing, Ronimund; Songs of Submission (James Clark 1962 and Altamira 1980)

von Bissing, Ronimund; Songs of the Heart (Altamira 1988)

Sources

The Editor would like to acknowledge the help of all the following, whether as contributors, correspondents, contacts or advisers:

Australia: Ismael Fido, Latif Lloyd, Katie Moss, David Nolde, Louis Patten, Harris Smart, Mardijah Simpson, Lavinia Swanson, Betty Wood, Rayner Young
Belgium: Faisal Sillem
Brazil: Raphael and Lorena Buyno
Canada: Rachael Crowder, Eirene Druce, Jan Duniewicz, Rosanna Hille, Rev Rohana Laing, Renata Morrison, Imbert Orchard
Colombia: Sac Olmedo de los Rios
Czechoslovakia: Mirko and Olga Schmid
North Cyprus: Hasan Fehmi
France: Patricia Auffret, Père Albert Bescond
Germany: Valentine Goebel, Harald Hoffman, Eberhard Lohss, Ludwig Mascher, Lilian Riedner, Lucie Schirren, Robert Schreiber
Great Britain and Ireland: Salah Ahmad, Alexandra Asseily, Anne Anderson, Roman Baszysinki, Deborah Bentin, Norah Bellis, Simon Blond, Joan Burrows, Adrienne and Dirk Campbell, Rev Charles Carey, Nicola Champness, Sheila Clarke, Betty Curtayne, Melinda Coulter, Rev Gideon Cox, Raphaelle Cuming, Leonard and Miriam Darlington, Robert Duveen, Roland and Orianne Evans, Joe Flynn, Fardijah Freedman, Maxwell Gibb, John Hager, Melinda Heathcote, Reynold Higginbottom, Howard Honeybone, Ruzêna Hyksova, Ridwan Isaacs, Dr Philip Jack, Ruslan and Hermine Jelmane, Margaret Johns, Lucas Kasta, Adrianna King-Hall, Martina Kingston, Michael Leach, Ronald Leask, Ilaine Lennard, Fredrik Lloyd, Marcus Mackay, Husein McGraw, Ruth Murray, Father Veda O'Kane, Leonard Oliver, Miriam Osborn, Helena Papps, Angela Powell, John Putnam, Violet Reiners, Victor Reynolds, Dominic Rieu, Richard Rashid and Dorotea Manar Rogers, James Robertson, Anneke Rynveld, Umar Salah, 'Salahuddin', Dunstan and Peata Savory, Hamid Michael Scott, Miriam Snow, Roland Store, Andrea Taylor, Antony Taylor, Rev James Tysoe, Wilbert Verheyen, Edith Waller, Isabel White, John Wilkens, John Williams, Marianne Wood
Indonesia: Harlinah Longcroft, Salamah Pope
Japan: Rozak Tatebe, Masaki Maru
Netherlands: Vivianne Baake, Edwin Gussenhoven

151

New Zealand: Jim and Miriam Holland
Norway: Helen Arberg, Raunie Hemsen, Prof Karsten Hundeide
Poland: Lydia Kzeminska, Kaziemierz Pomykala
Portugal: Robert Lyle
Romania: Traian and Gabriela Ocneanu
South Africa: Raymond Harper, Rainier Gebers, Lambert Kriedemann
Spain: Alberto Sanchez
USA: Simon Binnie, Rosada Cantrell, Roseanna Crouse, Reynold Feldman, Istvan Gorgenyi, Harlina Greenberg, Muhtar Holland, Levi Lemberger, Kathleen Mason, Rosalyn Neel, Miriam Ralph, Hasijah Rosefield, Renate and Garrett Thomson, Tarzie Varindra Vittachi, Dr Gisela Webb
Zaire: Nsimba Mampuya Rugasore

My sincere thanks to all of these, and to any whose names may have been left out; and especially to those who have supported the project all along, sometimes in the most practical of ways. I am specially grateful to my copy editor Adrienne Campbell for her patience, meticulous care and judgment as to what is fitting.